Skibbereen
THE FAMINE STORY

D1572153

Terri Kearney & Philip O'Regan

'Tree Sentinals' Famine memorial at Reen, by Susan O'Reilly. (Photo: A. Shaw)

Skibbereen
THE FAMINE STORY

Terri Kearney & Philip O'Regan

Foreword by
Grace Brady

Published in 2015 by:
Macalla Publishing,
Cunnamore,
Skibbereen, West Cork, Ireland.
macallapublishing@gmail.com

Macalla
Publishing

ISBN: 978-0-9926242-1-7

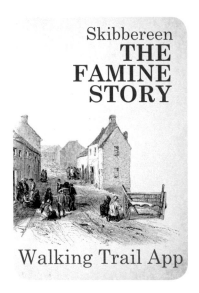

Skibbereen: *The Famine Story* app guides the walker through the sites and stories in Skibbereen town using the voices of the era. These include Dr Dan Donovan (portrayed by Fachtna O'Driscoll), R.B. Townsend (Peter Murray), Lord Dufferin (Jeremy Irons) and Elihu Burritt (Declan McCarthy). The app and its associated map can be downloaded on Skibbereen Heritage Centre's website, www.skibbheritage.com.

Please note that the majority of the sites mentioned in the book are accessible to the public. Only a few are on private property. The publication of this book allows these sites to be shared thanks to the goodwill and co-operation of the landowners but it does not suggest or promote the idea that these private sites can be visited. Please **respect the privacy** of these landowners and do not attempt to visit sites on private property without permission to do so.

Back page photo: Nikki Kitley
Sketches front/back: *Illustrated London News*

Design and layout: Southern Star, Skibbereen, www.southernstar.ie, 028 21200
Printed in Ireland.

CONTENTS:

Map of Skibbereen Union .... *vi*

Map of Skibbereen Town .... *viii*

Foreword by Grace Brady .... *xi*

Thanks and Acknowledgements .... *xii*

Introduction .... *xiv*

SKIBBEREEN: THE FAMINE STORY *1*
Before the Famine | **Potatoes** | **Poor Laws** | Workhouse | **1845—the Crisis Begins**
Relief Efforts | **Relief Works** | Myross Relief Scheme | First Official Death | **Skibbereen Committee**
Reports from Skibbereen | James Mahony | Gentlemen from Oxford | **Black '47** | International Relief
Government Soup | 1847 | **The 'End' of the Famine?** | Poor Laws Fail | **Disease**
Evictions | Evicting the Widow Ganey | **Emigration** | Australian Orphans | **Death** | Buried Alive

FAMINE: PEOPLE AND PLACES *69*
Harrington's Hut | Jeremiah O'Donovan Rossa | *Teampol na mBocht* | Schull Workhouse
Heir Island Shooting | Meinies | Ballydehob 1847 and Now | Schull 1847 and Now

POPULATION LOSS BY TOWNLAND *81*

THE FINAL WORD *83*

REFERENCES AND BIBLIOGRAPHY *85*

ABOUT THE CONTRIBUTORS *89*

The approximate location for the places mentioned in this book are shown here on this map. Many of the places referred to are general areas, for example headlands, townlands and lakes, so we have put an approximate location for these sites. Where an exact position has been identified, which is accessible to the public, the GPS for that site follows in brackets. Otherwise, the general area is marked on this map. More detailed maps will show the exact locations of these places. We would ask you to respect the privacy of the sites which are in private ownership.

1. Three Castle Head – page 5 - 6
2. Mizen Peninsula – page 8
3. Kilmoe Burial Ground – page 67 - 68, 79 (51.478474, -9.771935)
4. Crookhaven Village – page 74 (51.468233, -9.725227)
5. Dunmanus Townland – page 41
6. *Teampol na mBocht* (Altar Church) – page 73, 74 (51.519977, -9.642524)
7. Lowertown Townland – page 50
8. Gubbeen Townland – page 50, 79
9. Schull – page 45, 80: 63 Graveyard (51.519686, -9.546784), Workhouse 75, 84 (PRIVATE PROPERTY NO ACCESS)
10. Stouk burial grounds – page 64 (51.545498, -9.470432)
11. Ballydehob Village – page 55, 69, 79 (51.562627, -9.460765)
12. Skeaghanore Relief 'road to the sand quays at Reen' (51.550593, -9.426396) & Kilnaranna Cillín Skeaghanore – page xiiii, 63 (PRIVATE PROPERTY NO ACCESS)
13. Aughadown Parish – page 69, 70, 73, 76
14. Murrahin Townland – page 70
15. Kilcoe Relief Road, page v
16. Heir Island – page 76

17. Caheragh Parish – page 4, 21 - 22, 64
18. Meinies [Moyny Townland] Village – page 77, 78 (PRIVATE PROPERTY NO ACCESS)
19. Drimoleague Graveyard – page x and 64 (51.663083, - 9.262141)
20. Leitry Bridge – page 19 (51.695464, -9.265948)
21. Baltimore Village – page 56, 76 (51.483277, -9.37315)
22. Ballylinch Townland – page 41
23. Ballinard Townland – page 52
24. Highfield Townland – page 53, 54
25. Innisbeg Island – page 52
26. Creagh Townland – page 73
27. Lough Hyne lake – page 20
28. Tragumna Beach (and area) – page 16
29. Lick Townland – page 16
30. Marsh Road – page 16
31. Lisheennapingina Relief Road – page 16 (51.568746, -9.291007)
32. Farranagilla Townland – page 50
33. Reen Village – page ii, 25 (PRIVATE PROPERTY NO ACCESS)
34. Myross Townland – page 14, 15 , 17
35. Shepperton Lakes – page 27
36. Glandore Village – page 20
37. Rosscarbery Village – page 8, 20

Ballydehob

11

Schull

9

N7

5

7

8

6

10

16

Goleen

Heir Island

3

1

2

4

Cap

Skibbereen
THE FAMINE STORY

Skibbereen Union Area

20

18

19 · **Drimoleague**

17

N71

Rosscarbery

37

31

36 · **Glandore**

14

29

30

35

Union Hall

13

N71

Skibbereen

29

Castlehaven

33 34

32

26

25

24

27 28

21

23

22

Baltimore

erkin Island

Abbeystrowry Graveyard Pages 40, 62, 66 (51.551697, -9.287929)

N71

N71

Skibbereen
THE FAMINE STORY

Ilen Ri

P 10 9

Ilen St

8

Bridge St

7 6

Abbeystrewry
Pages 40, 44

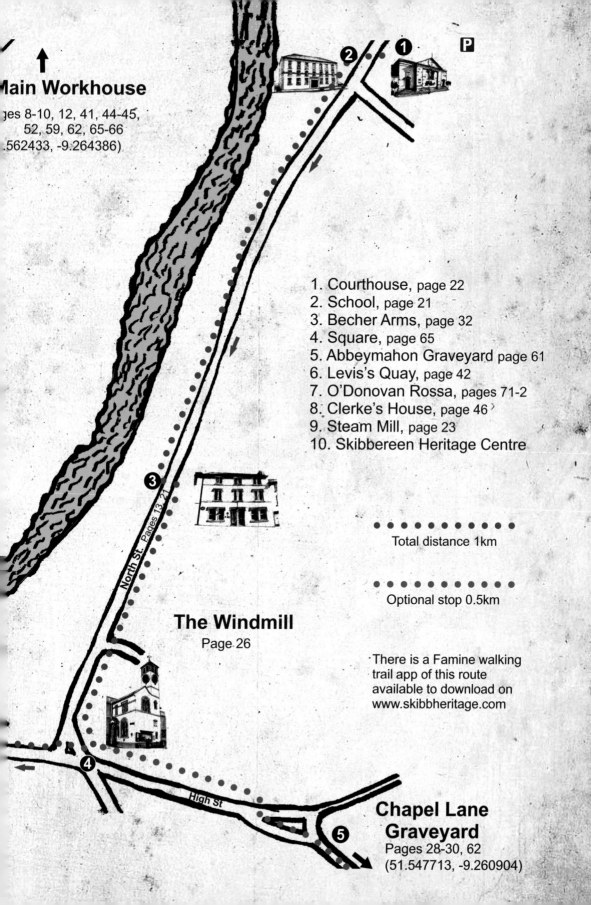

Main Workhouse

jes 8-10, 12, 41, 44-45,
52, 59, 62, 65-66
.562433, -9.264386)

1. Courthouse, page 22
2. School, page 21
3. Becher Arms, page 32
4. Square, page 65
5. Abbeymahon Graveyard page 61
6. Levis's Quay, page 42
7. O'Donovan Rossa, pages 71-2
8. Clerke's House, page 46
9. Steam Mill, page 23
10. Skibbereen Heritage Centre

North St. Pages 13-21

The Windmill
Page 26

Total distance 1km

Optional stop 0.5km

There is a Famine walking
trail app of this route
available to download on
www.skibbheritage.com

High St

Chapel Lane
Graveyard
Pages 28-30, 62
(51.547713, -9.260904)

FOREWORD

In February 1847 two remarkable men – one from Connecticut and one from Skibbereen – spent three harrowing days together among the dead and the dying. Elihu Burritt, the humanitarian from Connecticut, came to Cork to see for himself, and then share with the world what was happening to the poor people of Ireland during the fateful years of the Famine. Who better to reveal to him the true horror of events than Dr Daniel Donovan?

Almost one hundred and seventy years later, the Skibbereen Heritage Centre and Ireland's Great Hunger Museum at Quinnipiac University in Connecticut share a mission: to educate the public about the Great Hunger, the worst demographic catastrophe of nineteenth-century Europe. We in the Museum are honored to partner with Skibbereen in its commitment to informing the world of this horrific time in history, and we applaud its creative approach with the publication *Skibbereen: The Famine Story* which includes maps of Skibbereen and surrounding areas, as well as an accompanying Walking Trail App.

These initiatives authored by notable historians who are native to Skibbereen, Terri Kearney and Philip O'Regan, take us today over the ground covered by Burritt and Donovan, as the doctor ministered to the dying. The stories Donovan told Burritt about the people were brought back to America and narrated there in efforts to raise money to return to stricken Skibbereen.

The Heritage Centre's innovative audio guide takes visitors on a journey of remembrance through the most devastated areas in Skibbereen, sharing with them not only the unjust causes of the Great Hunger, but also the lasting consequences for its people, landscape and culture. The guide's narrative engages and compels those who listen to want to know more about this avoidable tragedy.

"I have seen how much beings, made in the image of God, can suffer on this side of the grave, and that too in a civilized land", lamented Burritt. We all must bear responsibility in continuing to educate others about this dark time in Ireland's history, so future generations can stand up to indifference in the fight to eradicate hunger in our time. We commend the Heritage Centre as it plays a central role in this endeavor, encouraging its visitors and the public at large to look back, in order to move forward in a beneficial way.

Grace Brady
Executive Director
Ireland's Great Hunger Museum at Quinnipiac University
Hamden, CT U.S.A.
May 2015

THANKS AND ACKNOWLEDGEMENTS

Both this publication and its associated app have required the help and assistance of many people. Particular thanks to our fellow contributors: Grace Brady of Ireland's Great Hunger Museum for her foreword, Reddy O'Regan for his photographs, Cecilia Scholte Lubberink for her sketches and map, and Mike Murphy of UCC for his support of the project and his superb maps.

We are very grateful to the many people who generously shared their properties and stories with us. Special thanks to Mary and Pat Hickey, Joan Woods and Richard Bradburn, Ann Shaw and Susan O'Toole, Séamus Newman, Marcie (Healy) Cassidy and Liz Cassidy, Kathleen and Vincent Keane, Tadhg O'Donovan, Denis and Teresa Shanahan, Janette Gerhard, Garry West and Peter, Geoff, Colin and Don Cummins.

We would like to acknowledge the fantastic research done on the Famine in this area by Fr Patrick Hickey as well Peter Foynes on behalf of the Skibbereen Famine Committee. We would also like to especially thank William Casey, Pat Cleary and Eugene Daly for their help and advice. Also the staff of the various libraries, especially Kieran Wyse and all in Cork County Library and Mary Lombard of the Boole Library.

As well as Reddy and Cecilia, many others contributed images to this publication. We would particularly like to thank the Crawford Art Gallery, Skibbereen Heritage Centre, Nikki Kitley, Ireland's Great Hunger Museum, Mike Murphy and the editors of the *Atlas of the Great Irish Famine,* UCC, the Ordnance Survey of Ireland, Desmond Leddin, the Irish Architectural Archive, John Sweeney and the Wales Famine Forum, Rob McAllen, Aughadown Parish, Seán Walsh, Trócaire and the National Portrait Gallery.

Many thanks to all who contributed their voices to the app, especially Jeremy Irons, Fachtna O'Driscoll, Declan McCarthy, Peter Murray, Gerald O'Brien, Stan Rispin and Derry Moynihane. Special thanks to Niall O'Driscoll for his patience and perfection in putting the recording together in such a professional way. Also to all the team at Sign Studio Skibbereen for their excellent work with the signage, especially Bob Clarke and Michał Ląkocy. To all the property owners who graciously allowed us to put up signs including Skibbereen Credit Union, Skibbereen Library, Ruth O'Brien of Cork County Council, Vicar John Ardis, Fr Michael Kelleher, Denis O'Leary, Edward and Paddy Nealon, Gerard Desmond, Tony Gibbons and Anne Cahalane. A special thanks to Mary Mulvihill and Vincent Hyland for their help and advice.

A huge thank you to the board of Skibbereen Heritage Centre for its support and to Mac Dara O h-Icí and Cork County Council. Also to the fantastic staff of the heritage centre, Margaret Murphy, Deirdre Collins, Maria Freeman and Elaine Deasy and to the 'unofficial staff', Patricia Tomlinson and William Casey. Thanks to all our proofreaders; John Earley, Tizzy Best, Kevin Tomlinson, Julianne Whooley and to our advisor on Irish spellings, Nuala Ní Bhriain and engineer Declan Groarke.

And a very special thanks goes to the talented Alan Tobin of *The Southern Star* for his superb design work and endless patience.

Our final acknowledgement is to those who suffered through the tragedy of the Great Famine in the Skibbereen Union. This book is in their honour. That they may always be remembered with compassion and respect.

Terri Kearney & Philip O'Regan

May 2015

Famine Relief Road 'to the Sand Quay', Skeaghanore. (Photo: R. O'Regan)

INTRODUCTION

The Great Irish Famine was the defining event in the history of modern Ireland. At least a million people died and double that number fled the country within a decade. It utterly transformed Ireland. Fifty years after the outbreak of the Famine, the population had halved.

Ireland lost more than its people. The social, cultural and psychological changes are harder to quantify but are equally as tragic. The Famine fundamentally changed both the land and the people of Ireland and distorted the course of Irish history.

The Skibbereen area played a very important role during the Great Famine. As the crisis unfolded, Skibbereen became infamous for the suffering of its people. The horrific reports from this area focussed worldwide attention on the progression of the disaster. The very name 'Skibbereen' became a byword for Famine.

Perhaps one of the saddest aspects of *an Gorta Mór* is the fact that millions of individual stories remain untold. No family in Ireland was unaffected by this enormous catastrophe but there are few accounts passed down over the generations. In a country that is celebrated for its musicians, artists and writers, such a traumatic event should feature prominently in the arts. However, the Great Famine was followed by a 'Great Silence' for well over a hundred years. The vast majority of the victims still remain unnamed.

The Famine is certainly not forgotten in West Cork. The Skibbereen Famine Committee has done fantastic work over the years in raising awareness about *an Gorta Mór* and an exhibition on the Famine is a permanent feature in Skibbereen Heritage Centre. Fr Patrick Hickey carried out comprehensive research for his excellent publication *Famine in West Cork*. Other local individuals and committees throughout the Skibbereen Union have also erected memorials to their Famine dead.

In *Skibbereen: The Famine Story,* our aim is to make this complex period accessible using contemporary reports of people and places in this area. Every individual story included here represents many thousands of others that remain untold, and the featured sites and locations serve as palpable links to these unnamed people. By telling what we know of their stories, we want to offer them the recognition and respect that was so lacking to them in life, and grant them peace.

our whitening bones ... will rise as witnesses,

From the cabins and the ditches, in their charred, uncoffin'd masses.

BEFORE THE FAMINE

The century before the Great Famine saw a huge population increase in Ireland. In 1750, the population was about two and a half million. Less than a hundred years later, on the eve of the Famine, it was well over 8.5 million people.[1] This was the highest population growth in Europe for that period.[2]

Because there was very little industry in Ireland at this time, the vast majority of the people were dependent on agriculture. So the landscape of Ireland would have looked very different to what it does today, with clusters of houses scattered throughout the countryside and small potato holdings all around. (*Illustrated London News, ILN*)

It was the poorest in society who were most affected by the Famine and their houses reflected their poverty. This 1847 sketch of houses in the Skibbereen Union shows how the poor lived. The fourth-class house, which was the lowest classification of housing in the 1841 census, was the living space for about 40% of the population in the Skibbereen area. (*ILN*)

The small, one-roomed fourth-class houses were built of stone or mud with a thatched roof and an earthen floor. Measuring between 3.6m (12 feet) and 4.5m (15 feet) wide internally, and of varying lengths, the poorest had no chimneys with the smoke escaping via the thatched roof. Windows were small and some cabins had a door only. In these dark cramped conditions, the family generally shared their living space with an animal, usually a pig, which was kept as a means of paying the rent.

The dependence on agriculture, alongside the rising population in Ireland, resulted in properties being divided and subdivided into smaller plots. Many landlords rented their land to a middleman, who, in turn, sublet it to tenant farmers and labourers. Everyone in this system paid rent, but the tenants of smallholdings paid a much higher rent proportionally than the middleman – or middlemen, as sometimes there was more than one involved. This graph is based on evidence given to the Devon Commission (1843–45) on examples of rents paid in the Skibbereen area. The increasing population and dependency on agriculture meant there was more demand for land. Rents in Ireland were very high as a result, between 80% and 100% higher than in England.[3]

POTATOES

Land use in Ireland changed significantly in the years before the Famine. The huge increase in population was built on agricultural output, with dependence on the potato increasing accordingly. This gradual shift from pastoral to tillage farming meant that each acre of land could support more people.

The potato was an ideal crop for the subsistence farmer. It could be grown on poor-quality land, requiring only a spade as a tool, and it was suitable for Ireland's weather conditions. It was also a very nutritious crop. With the addition of some buttermilk or fish, it provided all the requirements necessary for a healthy diet. However, the volumes required were huge, with a man eating up to 6.4kg (about 14lb) of potatoes each day.[1] Despite its monotonous nature, this was a relatively healthy diet. Irish men were taller than their British counterparts and life expectancy in Ireland was greater than in most European countries at that time.[2] ('The Potato Diggers in the West', 1903, by Charles McIver Grierson. Image courtesy of the Crawford Art Gallery.)

Because potatoes could be grown in poor-quality marginal land, an increase in their consumption meant more of the land of Ireland came under cultivation. Reclamation of previously untilled land, made possible by the robust nature of this crop, meant that bogs and uplands began to be used for growing potatoes.

The population increase was highest in areas where there was marginal, unenclosed land that could be newly colonised, primarily by young people. A large part of the area surrounding Skibbereen consisted of this kind of land. By the mid-1800s, Skibbereen Union was densely populated, with over 400 people to the square mile, in contrast to the average for Cork county of 200 to 300 per square mile.[3]

By 1845, more than half of the people in Ireland were directly dependent on the potato for their food, most especially the poor. The people who were most reliant on the potato had few other resources to fall back on and so were the most vulnerable in times of crop failure.

The Vicar of Abbeystrewry parish, Rev. R.B. Townsend, on the diet of the poor of Skibbereen: 'Potatoes their ordinary diet, sometimes with milk, sometimes with salt fish, and in dear seasons without either and alone'. The fishing industry in Ireland was largely underdeveloped at that time. While fish was abundant, fishermen were unable to afford the 'apparatus' to catch them and had no access to capital. The majority in West Cork still went to sea in skin-built boats called curraghs. Fishing was a precarious source of income and most of the fishermen in this area also had a small plot of ground to grow potatoes on which they were dependent. (*ILN*, 'Boy and Girl at Cahera' [sic])

Seed potatoes were planted in spade-dug drills, called 'lazy beds' and covered with earth. The potato could grow in the poorest conditions and, as the population continued to increase, marginal land began to be utilised. The traces of lazy bed cultivation shown here on Three Castle Head give an indication of the pressure for land that existed. These small pieces of ground, eked out between rock, are in a remote and inhospitable area on the Mizen peninsula at the edge of the Atlantic. (Photo: R. O'Regan)

POOR LAWS

After the 1800 Act of Union, Ireland did not have its own parliament and was governed directly from Westminster as part of the United Kingdom of Great Britain and Ireland. At the outbreak of the Famine, Ireland's population accounted for some 30% of the overall total of the British Isles.[1]

Ireland's poverty was seen as a potential threat to Britain's prosperity. It was feared that, should the disparity between the poor of Ireland and Britain grow too much, Britain would be flooded with Irish paupers as refugees.[2] Various inquiries into the conditions of the poor were carried out with a view to finding a solution.

Traditionally, poverty in Ireland was relieved almost entirely by private charity, with government intervention taking place only in times of extreme, sustained shortages. However, in 1838, a new system was put in place under the Poor Law of Ireland Act. The country was divided into 130 units, known as 'unions', each of which was to provide a workhouse for the relief of the poor. The Irish landowners were to fund the running of these workhouses.[3]

The Irish Poor Laws were modelled on the British system but with two important differences. Unlike Britain, relief was only to be given within the confines of the workhouse, as no 'outdoor relief' was permitted. Secondly, there was no 'right' to relief, so it was dependent on the availability of workhouse spaces.[4] These two clauses caused the deaths of many thousands of people during the Great Famine.

The principle of 'local chargeability' meant that each workhouse had to be supported by local ratepayers. By allocating the financial burden locally, landowners of the area would be 'encouraged' to take a greater interest in effectively managing their estates, resulting in a decreased demand for relief. This meant that, during the Great Famine, the worst affected areas had to support themselves financially.

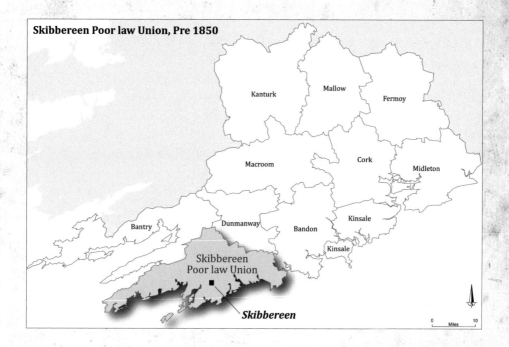

Skibbereen Poor law Union, Pre 1850

Kanturk

Mallow

Fermoy

Macroom

Cork

Midleton

Bantry

Dunmanway

Bandon

Kinsale

Skibbereen
Poor law Union

Kinsale

Skibbereen

0   Miles   10

Skibbereen Poor Law Union covered an area from Rosscarbery west to Mizen, a distance of some 65 kilometres (40 miles). The workhouse, situated just north of Skibbereen town, was to serve a population of 104,508. This large stone edifice was surrounded by high walls and dominated the entrance into the town, towering over the modest cabins and cottages that surrounded it. (Map: Mike Murphy, UCC)

Workhouse

A workhouse was a place where the destitute could go to exchange their labour for food. Skibbereen's workhouse was located just north of Skibbereen town, on the site now occupied by Skibbereen Community Hospital.

The workhouse system was designed so that only the desperate would avail of its services. It was established to provide support to the destitute, but its operation was closer to that of a prison service.

Individual people could not enter the workhouse, only entire family units. The rules required that these families be separated on admission, husbands from wives, parents from children.[5] The punitive nature of poor relief permeated all areas of life in the workhouse and applied to every inmate, including the elderly, infirm and children.[6]

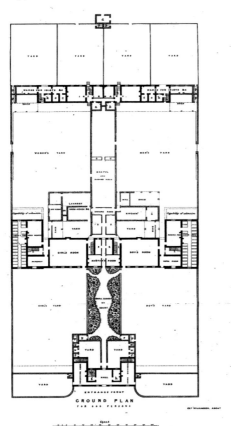

GROUND PLAN

The workhouse system was designed so that only the desperate would avail of its services. On entering the workhouse, families were split up with separate wards for men, women, boys, girls and young children. Modelled on the British system, as depicted in the tale of 'Oliver Twist', the regime was even stricter in Ireland where, unlike Britain, there was no 'right' to relief. (Image courtesy of the Irish Architectural Archive.)

Skibbereen workhouse opened in 1842 to serve a population of 104,508 people in the Skibbereen Union.[7] It was built to accommodate 800 people; however, at the height of the Great Famine, 3,784 desperate paupers sought refuge there.[8]

Workhouses were truly awful places and this one in Skibbereen was no exception. William Thackery wrote about it in 1842:

> as yet not more than 400 have been induced to live in it, the beggars preferring the freedom of their precarious trade to the dismal certainty within its walls.[9]

The Skibbereen Workhouse was burnt down in 1921 and all that remains of it today are the stone walls encircling the grounds of Skibbereen Community Hospital. These high forbidding walls are symbolic of the regime under which the workhouse operated. A burial ground dating to the Famine period is inside these walls. (Photo: T. Kearney)

1845 — THE CRISIS BEGINS

The potato blight, *Phytophthora infestans*, first affected the potato crop in north eastern America in 1843. Imported seed potatoes carried the disease across the Atlantic to Europe. It was first noticed in Cork city in the second week of September 1845. However, it was only when the potatoes were taken out of the ground in October that the full extent of the loss became apparent.

The late-maturing Lumper variety of potato, which was widely used in West Cork, was particularly badly affected by the new disease. Europe had no prior experience of this fungal infection which was spread rapidly by wind-borne infectious spores. Despite many efforts, no cure was found at that time.

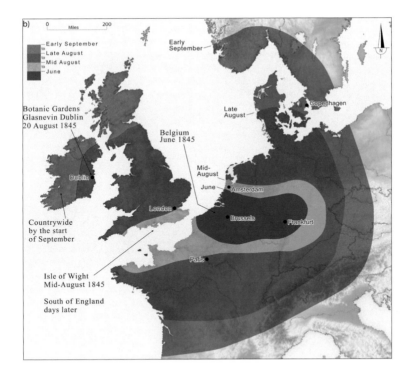

The new fungal disease spread throughout Europe causing widespread shortages. However, no other country was as reliant on this crop as Ireland. (Image courtesy of UCC and the editors of *Atlas of the Great Irish Famine*)

Dr Dan Donovan

Dr Dan Donovan was one of the most heroic figures of the Great Famine in Skibbereen. He was the first medical officer of the Skibbereen Workhouse and an exceptional physician. He worked in appalling conditions to help the diseased and dying people of Skibbereen without consideration for his own personal safety. He played a vital role in raising awareness about the unfolding crisis and the suffering of the people.

Dr Dan Donovan reported on 28 October 1845 that 'one-third of the entire crop was lost' in Skibbereen.[1]

The loss of the crop in 1845 was somewhere between a quarter and a third. However, the enormity of the crisis really only became apparent in 1846 when there was a 90% failure of the potato harvest.

Relief Efforts

The British Government, under Prime Minister Sir Robert Peel, set up a series of measures to alleviate the crisis. These were similar to those used in earlier famines in Ireland, but on a much larger scale. They involved the creation of work schemes so that the poor could earn money to buy food. The supply of food would be guaranteed by imports.

In 1845, Peel ordered the import from America of 'Indian Corn', or maize as we would call it today, to the value of some £100,000.[2] As this foodstuff was new to Ireland, it did not interfere with an established market. Peel's actions therefore conformed with the predominant economic principal of the time, known as *laissez-faire*. This advocated 'no [government] interference in the ordinary course of trade'.[3]

Peel's 'Indian Corn' was stored at depots all over Ireland. Skibbereen's store was located on the riverside of one of North Street's porches. The corn was to be sold at cost price to the local Relief committees to offset the huge rise in food prices caused by Famine inflation.

Exports of Irish food including meat, dairy and other commodities continued throughout the Famine.

Shipped, in good Order and Condition, by *the Myross Relief Com=* in and upon the good Ship or Vessel called the *Henry & Eliza* whereof *John Kelly* is Master for this present Voyage, and now riding at Anchor in the *Cork River* and bound for *Glandore*

Twenty four Sacks of Indian Meal. Containing Three Tons

being marked and numbered as in the Margin and are to be delivered in like good Order and Condition at the aforesaid Port of *Glandore* (the danger of the Seas, Fire, Rivers, and Navigation of whatsoever Nature and Kind excepted) unto *said committee* or to *their* Assigns, he or they paying Freight for the said Goods

Five shillings of Ton

with Primage and Average accustomed. In Witness whereof, the Master or Purser of the said Ship hath affirmed to *the* Bills of Lading, all of this Tenor and Date, one of which being accomplished, the other — to stand void.

Dated in *Cork* the 2 0 day of *May* 184 6

N.B.—By Sec. 34 of 5 and 6 Vic., cap 82, a Penalty of £50 is imposed for making or signing any Bill of Lading upon Unstamped Paper.—The Stamping a Bill of Lading when signed is prohibited.

John X Kelly / Myross
mark

24 Sacks of Flour

Indian W Smith

Myross Relief Committee, at a meeting held on 10 June 1846, ordered four tons of 'Indian Meal' for local relief. This arrived in Myross on 15 June 1846 on board the vessel *Galatea*. (Image courtesy of Marcie [Healy] Cassidy.)

The almost total potato crop failure in 1846 meant that, by August, all but a few food depots had run out of food. A new government, under Prime Minister John Russell, initially refused to import food. Finally, imports were authorised but long lead-in times, alongside a shortage of American maize in Europe, meant that the food could not arrive in time to avert deaths from starvation.

There was an extreme shortage of food that winter which resulted in an exponential rise in food prices. This meant that, by December 1846, a Skibbereen labourer earning the prevailing wage could not afford to buy enough food to feed a family. Many thousands of people slowly died of starvation during that bitterly cold winter.

RELIEF WORKS

The Famine relief work consisted of hard physical labour, often in bitterly cold weather, for a very low wage. Despite the hard work and difficult conditions, people were desperate to work on these schemes. By December, half a million people were working on relief works. When dependants are taken into account, this equates to roughly 2.5 million people receiving relief, while perhaps double that number were in terrible need.[1]

No._____

We, the undersigned, certify that from the best inquiries we have been able to make,

_____

has lost his Stock of Potatoes by the prevalent Disease, and is a proper object for employment on the Roads carried on by the Board of Works.

Dated at *(signature)* this 29th day of *August* 1846.

(signatures) } Members of Committee.

_____

By Authority—A. THOM, 87, Abbey-street, Dublin.

Local committees were given strict government guidelines on the requirements necessary to qualify to work on these schemes. Only the 'destitute' were granted tickets for work, such as this one from a relief road at Myross in the Skibbereen Poor Law Union. (Image courtesy of Marcie [Healy] Cassidy.)

The winter of 1846-47 was extreme, with severe frosts followed by heavy snowfall. Many of the public works had to be halted as a result and the workers were instead put to work breaking stones for a lesser wage.

As the Famine wore on, the poor pawned what few possessions they had. Fishermen pawned their nets but most people had to resort to surrendering their clothing. Dr Dan tells us in January 1847 that '40,000 pawn tickets, some representing 8 or 10 articles, have been issued within 3 months' in Skibbereen.[2]

This shortage of clothes exacerbated the appalling conditions on the relief schemes. A witness account from December 1846, graphically describes those working on the road works at Marsh Road, Skibbereen:

> At daybreak, I saw a gang of about 150, composed principally of old men, women, and little boys, going out to work ... At that time the ground was covered with snow, and there was also a very severe frost ... In the course of the day, I went out to visit this gang, who were opening a drain inside the fence on the Marsh road ... The women and children were crying out from the severity of the cold, and were unable to hold the implements with which they were at work, most of them declared that they had not tasted food for the day.[3]

Lisheennapingina Relief Road. In the Skibbereen area there were road works in Lick, Marsh Road, Tragumna and many other places including Lisheennapingina. Rev. R.B. Townsend described the workers on the latter scheme in 1847 as 'unfortunate creatures without shoe or stocking, actually perishing as they stood, from cold, hunger and exhaustion'.[4] (Photo: R. O'Regan)

NAMES OF THE WORKERS ON THE MYROSS RELIEF SCHEME, 28 AUGUST 1846. (As recorded.)

(with thanks to Deirdre Collins and Margaret Murphy)

From Ardagh: Denis Mahony, Michael Coughlan, Daniel Coughlan, John Collins, Daniel Driscoll, Michael Driscoll, Pat Hayes, John Dwire, Daniel Collins, James Collins, Jeremiah Dwire, Richard Nagle, Michael Nagle, Cornelius Collins, Daniel Dawly, Jeremiah Dwire, Jer Walsh, Denis Dwyer.

From Ardrah: Daniel Daly, Michael Buee, John Daly.

From Ballinatona: Denis Donovan, Patrick Fitzgerald, John Burke, Michael Driscoll, Joseph Donovan, Michael Savage.

From Ballincolla: Patrick Regan, Michael Canty, John Canty, Pat Driscoll.

From Bawnlahan: Richard Connell.

From Brade: Tim Collins, Denis Crimeen, Michael Donovan, Jeremiah Hegarty, Richard Burchill, Thomas Harrington, J. Casey, (not employed), Paddy Donovan, Phil Donovan, Jerry Donovan, Richard Casey, Jer Sullivan, John Mahony, Jer Crowley, John Harrington.

From Cahergal: Daniel Walsh.

From Castle Ire (Castle Island?): John Croston, John Dwyer, Jeremiah Connolly, Patrick Hayes.

From Carrigillihy: Jeremiah Carty, Cornelius Neal, Denis Walsh, Denis Hennessy, John Leary, Jeremiah Murray, Timothy Driscoll, Jerry Wholey, Daniel Horan, Timothy Meenig, Cornelius Donovan, Jeremiah Donovan, Michael Donovan, James Sullivan, Daniel Donovan, Charles Glaveen, Michael Greany, Denis Greany, Denis Donovan, Timothy Donovan, Pat Hegarty, Tim Sullivan, Jer Carty, Cornelius Neal, Denis Walsh, Denis Hennessy, John Leary, Jeremiah Murray, Timothy Driscoll, Jerry Wholey, Daniel Horan, Timothy Meenig, Cornelius Donovan, Cornelius Donovan, Jeremiah Donovan, Michael Donovan, James Sullivan, Daniel Donovan(Greany), Charles Glaveen, Michael Greany, Denis Greany, Denis Donovan, Timothy Donovan, Pat Hegarty, Tim Sullivan, Cornelius Callaghan, Richard Meenig, James Tobin, Jeremiah Driscoll, Morgan Donovan, Denis Glavin, Jeremiah Murray, Cornelius Greany, Michael Sullivan, Daniel Donovan, William Casey, Daniel Horen, Richard Walsh, Patrick Collins, Cornelius Hegarty, Timothy Driscoll, Jerry Donovan, Daniel Leary, John Collins, Pat Collins, Jeremiah Greany, Jer Sullivan, John Murray, Daniel Greany, Cors Hegarty, Jeremiah Daly, Andres Carthy, Timothy Donovan, Cors Greany, Daniel Greany, Daniel Collins, John Collins, Jerry Hegarty, Timothy Donovan, Denis Glaveen, William Sullivan(?), Cornelius Donovan, Timothy Hegarty, Jerry Driscoll, Michael Walsh.

'his death was caused from dire necessity and want of food. His name was Denis Driscoll, and he worked on the Myross road to which he was obliged to walk three miles every day, and return at night to his family.' *SR*, 19 January 1847

'a poor man named Paddy Whelton ... died this morning near Myross demesne gate from the combined effects of cold and hunger ... he was working on the Myross road.' *SR*, 19 January 1847

| Carrigillihy. (Photo R. O'Regan)

From Clontaff: John Cleary, Tim Collins, Michael Collins, John Driscoll, Francis Cotter, Pat Donoghue, John Driscoll, James Collins, Daniel Donovan, Cornelius Driscoll, David Regan.

From Cooldurragha: Daniel Connolly, Henry Casey, William Casey, Jer Collins, Michael Wholey, Richard Browne, Jeremiah Connell.

From Cooscroneen: Denis Collins, Cors McSweeney, Daniel Burke, Laurence Daly.

From Kippagh: John White.

From Listarkin: Jerh Sullivan, Jerh Daly, Jerh Donovan, Denis Donovan, Jas Walsh, William Daly, James Sullivan, Denis Donovan, David Donovan, Daniel Buee, John Finn, Owen Sullivan, John Donovan, John Horan, James Sweeny, Denis Donovan, Michael Donovan, Timothy Rogers.

From Maulicarrane: Pat Wholey.

From Myross: Michael Houlahan, Dan Keating, William Simmons, William Keating, John Brien, Daniel Cronin, John McCarthy.

From Raheen: John Donovan, Daniel Mahony.

From Reen : Patrick Hegarty, Denis Regan, Pat Minihane, Pat Carthy, John Dwyer, Michael Buckley, Jerh Driscoll.

From Rhea: Jerry Carthy.

From Scahanagh : Thomas Hurley, John Meenig, Michael Driscoll, Denis Greany, Timothy Hennessy, Daniel Crowley, John Meenig, John Crowley, Jer Driscoll.

From Union Hall: Bryan Sweeny, James Sweeny, Michael Hurley, Daniel Murphy, Daniel Burke, John Kelly, Timothy Burke, Michael Donovan, Jer Connor, Michael Hennessy, Timothy Dawly, John Dwire, John Donoghue, Daniel Donovan Tragh, Florence Driscoll, John Dwyer, Pat Minihane.

| (Image courtesy of Marcie [Healy] Cassidy.)

From September 1846 onwards, a scheme based on task labour, or 'piece work', came into effect on the relief works, replacing the former daily wage.[5] The amount paid had to be lower than the usual local wage in order to avoid the risk of encouraging 'unscrupulous conduct'.[6] This system pushed those least able for physical activity, such as the ill and the elderly, below the level of subsistence.

Many thousands of people employed on these public works slowly died of starvation in the winter of 1846-47. Malnourished or sick, they were unable to earn enough under the measured task system of labour to buy sufficient food to stay alive. Even when there was money to pay for it, there was often no supply of food available. The works brought together large numbers of malnourished people and thus facilitated the spread of diseases which were, by this stage, reaching epidemic proportions.

Leitry Bridge near Drimoleague, also in Skibbereen Union, was built as a relief effort during the Great Famine. Many people died of starvation and 'road sickness' while working on such schemes. In a malnourished and weakened condition, they were extremely susceptible to disease. The relief works brought large numbers of these people together, thereby facilitating the spread of the 'fever'. (Photo: R. O'Regan)

'About 30 or 40 unemployed labourers drove off the men at work on this line of road between Glandore and Ross this day, and said they would not allow them to return except they were employed themselves. I have ordered such of them as may be known to be summoned and this morning about 80 unemployed men passed through the village of Glandore with spades and shovels, seemingly in much distress, looking for work but committed no violence.'[7]

Despite the many deaths, the low wages and appalling conditions, people were desperate for work on the relief schemes.

The wall of 'The Rapids' at Lough Hyne was built as a Famine relief scheme in early 1847. This was a bitterly cold winter and the workers on the scheme would have had to stand in the freezing waters of the Lough to build this wall.[8] (Photo: R. McAllen)

First Official Death

The relief works were a massive undertaking driven by a bureaucratic monstrosity. Decisions on eligibility and rates of pay came from London and the rules were constantly being changed. It was a logistical nightmare that resulted in many administrative errors, including frequent delayed payment of wages.

On Wednesday 30 September 1846, between 800 and 1,000 desperate men, workers on the Caheragh Road relief scheme, marched into Skibbereen to protest about late-payment of their wages.

Dr Dan Donovan was riding into Skibbereen from the country and passed the men as they marched into the town. Dr Dan warned the townspeople of their approach:

> those once stalwart men but now emaciated spectres ... marched along, bearing upon their shoulders their ... spades, shovels etc ... in the glitter of a blazing sun.[9]

Skibbereen prepared for a riot and some 75 soldiers gathered in North Street to halt the men's progress into the town.

A local Justice of the Peace, Michael Galwey, intervened and some food was distributed. The demonstration lasted for about four hours despite Galwey's appeals for the men to disperse. This dangerous situation was eventually diffused and the men returned to Caheragh.[10]

This 1847 sketch shows the site of the Caheragh men's protest. The road into Skibbereen from the north ran behind this large building, which was then a school. In 1846, soldiers assembled there, their guns primed and loaded, to halt the Caheragh men's approach into town. *(ILN)*

One of the first deaths of the Famine in Ireland was of a man working on the Caheragh Relief Works. Denis McKennedy died on Saturday 17 October, just days after the Caheragh men's protest march. We don't know if Mr McKennedy was one of the men who marched into Skibbereen that day but his inquest found that he had 'died of starvation, caused by the gross negligence of the Board of Works'.[11]

The inquest heard that Mr McKennedy had not been paid in weeks. An administrative error made by the pay clerk of the Board of Works, T.J. Hungerford Esq., had cost Mr McKennedy his life.

Denis McKennedy was one of the first of the many thousands of people who died on the relief works over the following months.

The inquest into the death of Denis McKennedy was held in the courthouse directly across from the school shown on the opposite page. (*ILN*)

SKIBBEREEN COMMITTEE

By late 1846 the poor of Skibbereen were dying on the streets, in their homes and on the relief works. A group of local individuals came together in an effort to alleviate their suffering and formed the Skibbereen Committee of Gratuitous Relief. On 7 November 1846, this committee opened one of the first large-scale soup kitchens in Ireland.[1]

The Skibbereen committee fed up to 8,600 people every day from the Steam Mill building in Ilen Street.[2] We have descriptions of those who went there for soup, including this one from February 1847:

> The soup-house was surrounded by a crowd of these famine-spectres ... [the entrance] was choked with young and old of both sexes, struggling forward with their rusty tin and iron vessels for soup, some of them upon all fours, like famished beasts.[3]

As well as dispensing soup from the Steam Mill building, the Skibbereen Committee of Gratuitous Relief also distributed food to areas outside of the town. This was an attempt to halt the flood of people pouring into the town in search of aid. In February 1847 alone, over 3,000 came into Skibbereen looking for relief. The committee sent soup and rice 'in closed barrels by carts, distances of 3, 4, 5 miles to the country in different locations [as well as] rice milk daily sent round to the sick'.[4] (Photo: T. Kearney)

A member of the Skibbereen Committee of Gratuitous Relief, Rev. R.B. Townsend, travelled to London in November 1846 seeking relief for Skibbereen. He and another local vicar, Rev. Charles Caulfield, met with Charles Edward Trevelyan, Assistant Secretary to the Treasury. Just three days later, Trevelyan requested that a portion of the 'Ceylon subscription' be sent to Skibbereen 'where, judging from the number of deaths, the destitution must be frightful'.[5] The vicars sought to 'procure a Queen's letter; an instrument of authority for collections being made in the national churches'.[6] The Queen subsequently did write a letter of appeal and the church collection brought in £171,533 in aid to Ireland.[7]

Charles Edward Trevelyan strongly influenced government policy during the Great Famine. He was an ideologically driven workaholic who was a strong supporter of the *laissez-faire* economic doctrine. He believed that Ireland's pre-Famine conditions and 'social evil' were altered by an 'all-merciful' God.[8] In his eyes, the Famine was a punishment sent by God that had to take its course, and any human intervention would therefore be contravening His divine will. Trevelyan's policies, which reflected the economic beliefs of the period, exacerbated the effects of the Famine and caused untold suffering and mortality. However, he was lauded by his contemporaries and, in 1848, was knighted for his work in Ireland.[9] (Charles Edward Trevelyan by John Watkins, National Portrait Gallery, London.)

In the written accounts of the time, the desperation of the people is tangible. Hoards of starving people were moving about in search of food, with none to be had. The situation was worsening by the day and reports of suffering in the Skibbereen Poor Law Union began to appear in the media. The *Cork Examiner* and another Cork newspaper, the *Southern Reporter*, carried extensive coverage of the Famine in the Skibbereen area under such headlines as 'Death by Starvation', 'More Deaths from Starvation!!!', 'Another Death by Starvation', 'More Deaths by Starvation'.[10]

REPORTS FROM SKIBBEREEN

Nicholas Cummins, a Justice of the Peace from Cork city, visited Skibbereen in December 1846 to witness the effects of the Famine. What he saw shocked him. He wrote a harrowing letter to the Duke of Wellington which was published on the front page of *The Times* newspaper on Christmas Eve 1846.

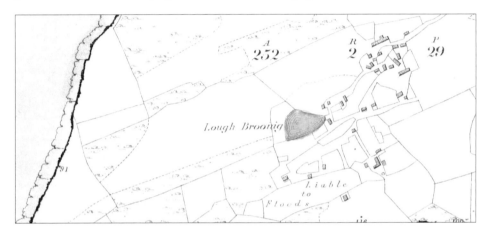

Reen Village as it appeared in the 1842 OS map of Ireland. Cummins gave us this description of the village in 1846: 'I was surrounded by at least 200 of such phantoms, such frightful spectres as no words can describe. By far the greater number were delirious, either from famine or fever. Their demoniac yells are still yelling in my ears and their horrible images are fixed upon my brain'.[1] (© Ordnance Survey Ireland/ Government of Ireland. Copyright Permit No. MP 001615)

All that remains of Reen village today is the road shown here. 'Out of 62 houses, and 320 inhabitants, on the farm of South Reen, two years since, there now remain, after the ravages of disease and poverty, *but 8 hovels, and about 50 people*; the houses were pulled down for firing, and the people carried off by fever. At this moment I have no doubt but dead bodies are putrefying beneath the remains of the deserted huts'.[2] (Photo: R. O'Regan)

Cummins also related many scenes of death and disease that he witnessed in Skibbereen. In one, he said that Dr Dan Donovan 'found seven wretches lying, unable to move, under the same cloak. One had been dead for many hours, but the others were unable to move either themselves or the corpse'.[3]

We have many accounts from Dr Dan Donovan regarding the appalling conditions in Skibbereen. He visited tiny cottages and hovels where the starving and diseased were dying.

Foundations of houses, cut into rock, which were occupied during the Famine, can still be seen today on the Windmill Rock in Skibbereen. This was one of the worst affected areas of the town during the Great Famine.

We have this report from Dr Dan from the Windmill on 27 December 1846: 'In a nook in this miserable cabin … a green and ghastly corpse that had been for five days dead … at the feet of this decomposing body lay a girl groaning with pain; and by its side was a boy frantic in fever. The wife of the deceased sat upon the filthy floor stupefied from want and affliction. I asked her in the name of Heaven why she did not get her husband buried, her answer was she "had no coffin." I enquired why she did not go out and look for one; decency would not allow her, for she was naked; the few rags that she had after the fever had rotted off her, and she hoped that a coffin would be her next dress.'[4] (Photo: T. Kearney)

James Mahony

By early 1847, Skibbereen was being referred to as the 'very nucleus' of the Famine.[5] Many overseas visitors came to Skibbereen in order to witness and report on the crisis.

James Mahony of the newspaper the *Illustrated London News* visited Skibbereen in early 1847. Mahony sketched famine scenes from the Skibbereen Poor Law Union and these images appeared alongside his reports. The Skibbereen area featured in the *Illustrated London News* on 30 January, 13 February and 20 February 1847. Mahony's descriptions were graphic and by using terms such as 'I saw', 'I heard' and 'I met', he identified himself as an eyewitness to the tragedy.

FUNERAL AT SHEPPERTON LAKES.

Mahony sketched many funerals during his visit to Skibbereen Poor Law Union in 1847, including this one at Shepperton, near Leap. These illustrations were considered truly shocking at the time. Contemporaneous art depicting such terrible events was more or less unprecedented before the Great Famine.[6] (*ILN*)

THE HUT OR WATCH-HOUSE IN THE OLD CHAPEL YARD.

James Mahony's sketch of the 'Watch-house' at Chapel Lane Graveyard, in the *Illustrated London News* of 13 February 1847, was accompanied by this account from Dr Donovan about the Barrett family:

> Six members of one family, named Barrett, who had been turned out of the cabin in which they lodged, in the neighbourhood of Old Chapelyard ... had struggled to this burying-ground, and literally entombed themselves in a small watch-house ... This shed is exactly seven feet long, by about six in breadth. By the side of the western wall is a long, newly-made grave; by either gable are two of shorter dimensions, which have been recently tenanted; and near the hole that serves as a doorway is the last resting-place of two or three children; in fact, this hut is surrounded by a rampart of human bones, which have accumulated to such a height that the threshold, which was originally on a level with the ground, is now two feet beneath it. In this horrible den, in the midst of a mass of human putrefaction, six individuals, males and females, labouring under most malignant fever, were huddled together, as closely as were the dead in the graves around. (*ILN*)

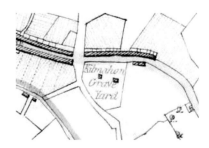

This 1842 map of Chapel Lane Graveyard shows the location of the old church to the right and the watch-house, described here, in the centre of the graveyard. (© Ordnance Survey Ireland/Government of Ireland. Copyright Permit No. MP 001615)

'Funeral at Chapel Lane' as depicted by James Mahony in 1847 and the same scene today.(*ILN* & R. O'Regan)

Gentlemen from Oxford

In February 1847, two young students at Oxford University, Lord Dufferin and the honourable G.F. Boyle, came to Skibbereen. They brought £50 with them which had been raised by the students at Oxford for Famine relief in Ireland.

Their letter dated 1 March 1847 said that:

> The accounts are not exaggerated – they cannot be exaggerated – nothing more frightful can be conceived. The scenes we have witnessed during our short stay at Skibbereen equal anything that has been recorded by history, or could be conceived by the imagination. Famine, typhus fever, dysentery and a disease hitherto unknown, are sweeping away the whole population.[7]

Dufferin and Boyle were given this account by Dr Donovan:
> At some distance from Skibbereen there was a cottage, in which lay a man and his wife both sick of the fever; the woman died, and the husband had just sufficient strength to crawl out and bury the body in his garden. During the night he distinctly heard dogs scratching and howling over what he but too well knew was the lately made grave; he sent out his little girl to drive them away, but they only bit at her, and frightened her back into the cottage. The following day one of the neighbours brought back the head of the unfortunate woman, saying 'that his dog had brought it home!'[8]

Dufferin and Boyle stayed in the Becher Arms Hotel in North Street (the building is now divided in two). On the morning of their departure from Skibbereen, the two young men purchased a huge basket of bread to distribute to the poor. Their shopping did not go unnoticed and a large crowd assembled at the hotel: 'It was a frightful sight to see these pale eager faces staring up at us, uttering all manner of entreaties … At first we sent [the bread] down to the door, but the rush was so great, that that scheme became impracticable; and it only remained to throw it out of the window. One can never forget what followed; the fighting, the screaming, the swaying to and fro of the human mass, as it rushed in the direction of some morsel'.[9] (Photo of the building as it is today by Nikki Kitley.)

On their return to Oxford, Dufferin and Boyle published a pamphlet about their visit, *Narrative of a Journey from Oxford to Skibbereen During the Year of the Irish Famine*. The proceeds of this work were to be sent for Famine relief in Skibbereen.

Shortly afterwards, another Famine donation of £1,000 was also directed to Skibbereen. Given by an unidentified 'Irish Landlord', it was learned many years later that Lord Dufferin was this anonymous donor.[10]

BLACK '47 — *International Relief*

In the early months of 1847, a huge amount of aid flowed into Ireland from all over the world. From the Choctaw Nation in America to the Sultan of Turkey, 'contributions from every part of the compass, in money and food ... poured in'.[1]

The horrific reports about the Famine in Skibbereen were the catalyst that led to the establishment of the 'British Association for the Relief of Extreme Distress in the remote parishes of Ireland and Scotland'.[2] This Association was the conduit for much of the international aid, raising almost £400,000 for relief in Ireland.[3]

The British public's response to the crisis was overwhelming, ranging from a shilling given by 'a poor man' to the £2,000 donated by Queen Victoria.[4] Many individual subscriptions from all over Britain were sent directly to Skibbereen.

The visit of the American philanthropist Elihu Burritt, and his subsequent publication *Three Days in Skibbereen and its Neighbourhood*, also played an important role in bringing aid into Ireland. His graphic descriptions of this area raised general awareness in America (particularly outside of the Irish community) about the Famine and greatly helped relief efforts there.

The relief effort for Ireland in the winter of 1846-7 was a truly international one. However, these international relief efforts undoubtedly embarrassed the politicians of Britain. At a time when one in four of the world's population was ruled from London, this international aid undermined the concept of the Empire as a great economic and political power.[5]

THE CORK SOCIETY OF FRIENDS SOUP HOUSE.

The Quakers formed a relief committee in November 1846 and began to open soup kitchens. During the course of the Famine, they channelled relief valued at around £200,000 into Ireland, primarily as food shipments from the United States.[6] The Society of Friends also played a huge role in publicising the Famine and its horrific consequences. (*ILN*)

Government Soup

Pressure mounted on the British government to take action and, in early 1847, the 'soup kitchen act' was hurried through parliament. Its intention was to deliver cheap food to the masses via soup kitchens while simultaneously winding down the public works.

Like the road relief works, the diktats for the operation of the soup kitchens came from London and required a massive administrative bureaucracy which took months to establish. This system of relief was intended to be only a temporary measure, lasting until the harvest season of 1847 when a revised Poor Law system would come into place.[7]

The soup kitchen system was much cheaper to run than the public works; but the emphasis was, at all times, on cutting down costs and the possibility of abuse. The numbers of people in receipt of soup steadily increased and, by July 1847, over three million people were fed from the soup kitchens each day.[8] This measure worked and the deaths from starvation were arrested, however disease still raged.

Tickets for soup at a soup kitchen. Rigid rules, aimed at keeping down costs, controlled the provision of soup from these government-run kitchens. One of the recipes, known as 'Soyer's Soup', had just a quarter pound of beef in two gallons of water while the Quakers' soup contained six times that amount.[9]

1847

It was a dry summer in 1847 so there was little blight. However, there was only a small harvest. Because of the shortage of food in 1846, no seed potatoes had been kept to plant for the following year. With seed being very scarce and expensive, the potato acreage planted in 1847 was only around one seventh of what it had been the previous year.[10]

THE ENGLISH LABOURER'S BURDEN;

Or, THE IRISH OLD MAN OF THE MOUNTAIN.

[See *Sinbad the Sailor.*

By this stage of the Famine, sympathy for Ireland was wearing thin and the British media reports of the time reflect this 'famine fatigue'. Attacks on Irish landlords and the Irish land system were widespread and, according to the critics, Irish landlords had been so neglectful of their duties that they had created the conditions that led to the Famine. Worse again, they were dumping their evicted pauper tenants on the shores of England, Scotland and Wales.[11] A severe financial crisis in Britain further exacerbated the situation. (*Punch*. Image courtesy of Ireland's Great Hunger Museum, Quinnipiac University, Hamden, CT.)[12]

The Poor Law Amendment Act was passed in June 1847, before the outcome of that year's harvest was known. This Act shifted the burden of providing relief from the British Treasury onto the Irish landlords and tenants. The British government had always considered the soup kitchens to be a temporary measure, to last only until the harvest of 1847, and all of the government-run soup kitchens closed in September 1847.[13]

1847 relief figures for the parishes that encompassed Skibbereen town[14]

	Population in 1841	Max. number of people given relief in any one day	Date relief started	Date relief finished	No. of people on the list when relief measures stopped
Creagh parish	6415	4864	26 May 1847	12 Sept. 1847	916
Tullagh parish	4742	3531	27 May 1847	2 Sept. 1847	561

The relief measures under the 1847 Temporary Relief Act for the two parishes that surrounded Skibbereen town shows the numbers in receipt of soup. Over 70% of people in Creagh and Tullagh received relief on the busiest day.[15] There were still 916 people on this list in Creagh and 561 in Tullagh when 'the supply of rations ceased'.[16] The last report of the Relief Commissioners notes that during the period of relief:

The orderly and good conduct of the peasantry ... is highly to be commended. All admit that resignation and forbearance of the labouring classes was astonishing.[17]

An insight into the thinking of the official administration of the time comes from Trevelyan's book, *The Irish Crisis*, published in autumn 1847:

> In the west and south of Ireland ... the owners and holders of land ... had permitted or encouraged the growth of the excessive population which depended on the precarious potato ... [the blight was the hand of God as] ... Supreme Wisdom had educed permanent good out of transient evil.[18]

THE

IRISH CRISIS.

BY

C. E. TREVELYAN, Esq.

REPRINTED FROM THE "EDINBURGH REVIEW."

No. CLXXV., January, 1848.

LONDON:
LONGMAN, BROWN, GREEN & LONGMANS.
1848.

The Famine was seen to be a judgement sent by God to sort out Ireland's long-standing problems. The way in which the Irish landlords were treated by the British press and parliament during this time displays the telltale features of scapegoating and, with God's judgement added to the equation, it helped to resolve any British middle-class guilt about the mass deaths.[19]

THE IRISH CRISIS.

THE time has not yet arrived at which any man can with confidence say, that he fully appreciates the nature and the bearings of that great event which will long be inseparably associated with the year just departed. Yet we think that we may render some service to the public by attempting thus early to review, with the calm temper of a future generation, the history of the great Irish famine of 1847 *. Unless we are much deceived, posterity will trace up to that famine the commencement of a salutary revolution in the habits of a nation long singularly unfortunate, and will acknowledge that on this, as on many other occasions, Supreme Wisdom has educed permanent good out of transient evil.

* We have endeavoured to gather up all the threads of this strange tissue, so that every circumstance of importance connected with the measures of relief may be placed on record; but our narrative does not, except in a few instances, extend beyond September 1847, and the progress of events after that date will form the subject of a separate article. B

THE 'END' OF THE FAMINE?

After the closure of the soup kitchens in September, the Outdoor Relief system came into operation. This meant that people could get food through the Poor Laws without going into a workhouse. This was initially limited to the 'non-able bodied' but later extended to all. However, to gain entitlement to it, the able-bodied poor had to break stones for ten hours a day.[1]

Outdoor Relief had always been part of the poor law system in Britain but was not included in the Irish Poor Laws of the late 1830s. This was because the government of the time was advised that its provision was impossible in the Irish situation, as the demand would swamp property owners.[2] Yet these same rate payers, by now in their third year of famine, were deemed capable of providing it to millions of starving people in 1847.

| (ILN)

There was an overwhelming demand for Outdoor Relief. More than 5,300 people were on the lists of the Skibbereen Union for Outdoor Relief in November 1848, with at least 3,100 more in the workhouse.[3] By April 1849, the numbers had risen to a staggering 3,784 in the workhouse and 15,748 on the list for Outdoor Relief.[4]

In effect, the British government declared the Famine to be 'over' in 1847 when it decreed that 'Irish property must pay for Irish poverty'. The government's decision to throw the whole burden of relief on to Irish landlords, who were already in a crisis state, was a death sentence for many thousands of Irish people.[5]

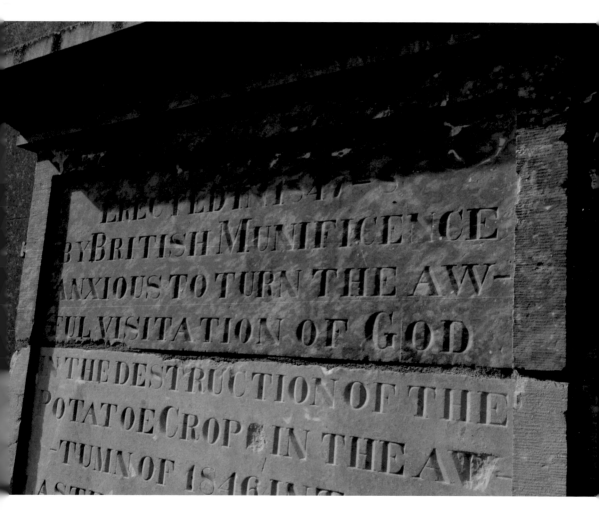

This plaque on the exterior wall of Abbeystrewry Church was erected by its parishioners in the winter of 1847-8 in thanksgiving 'for their rescue from the horrors and suffering of the Famine'. They clearly believed that the crisis was over then. However, the death of their vicar, R.B. Townsend, in 1850 showed that it was far from over. (Photo: P. O'Regan)

Poor Laws Fail

With the closure of the soup kitchens, the sole system of relief from 1847 onwards was through the workhouses, which were hopelessly underfunded and overcrowded. Skibbereen Union Workhouse, built to cater for 800 people, contained 2,757 inmates in November 1848.[6] By April 1849, this number had swollen to 3,784.[7]

Many desperate people travelled long distances into the town, only to find that the workhouses were full when they got there. Fr Fitzpatrick, Catholic priest in Skibbereen, told us that they came from:

> the most remote parts of the Union ... hundreds of the most destitute human beings ... some of them spent days on their journey to Skibbereen, fainting with hunger, crawling along the roads, for they were not ... able to walk, and when they reached the poorhouse they were told there was no room ... they were obliged to sleep in the dung in the poorhouse stables ... or in the open air, in the fields and streets of Skibbereen ... Katy Cody of Dunmanus ... travelled 30 miles, was refused admittance, there being no room, slept in the streets ... and walked back ... Ellen O'Driscoll of West Ballylinch ... travelled 63 miles and got no relief.[8]

some of them spent days on their journey to Skibbereen, fainting with hunger, crawling along the roads, for they were not ... able to walk

A number of auxiliary workhouses were opened to try and cater for the flood of poor people that crowded into the town in search of aid.

One of these emergency workhouses, Swanton's Store, was situated on Levis's Quay. It was mentioned by A.G. Stark, in his *Journal* of 1850:

> I did not visit any of the poorhouses; indeed, the shrill sound of female voices that reached my ear, as I passed one of them – Swanstone's [*sic*] Stores – as if nothing reigned within except discord and pain – rendered the invitation to enter anything but desirable.[9]

nothing reigned within except discord and pain

| 'Swanton's Store' before it was demolished in February 2005. (Photo: P. O'Regan)

DISEASE

Disease was a major cause of death during the Great Famine. The term 'famine fever' covered a range of diseases but the worst of these were typhus and relapsing fever. Both were transmitted by the human body louse.

Famine conditions facilitated the spread of disease. Huge numbers of poor, malnourished people congregated in cities and towns in search of aid from 1846 onwards. The road relief works and the soup kitchens also brought large crowds together. And, of course, the overcrowded workhouses also provided optimum conditions for the spread of disease.

Relapsing fever caused vomiting and was often accompanied by jaundice, hence its other name — yellow fever.

Typhus was also known as black fever as it affected the blood circulation and made the patient's face swell up and darken.[1]

Relapsing fever was prevalent among the poor, while typhus also affected the higher social classes, particularly those who were engaged directly in relief work.

Rev. R.B. Townsend, Vicar of Abbeystrewry parish, contracted typhus at Skibbereen Workhouse, and died from it in 1850.[2] Townsend was very active in seeking relief for the poor of Skibbereen and paid for it with his life. There is a plaque to his memory erected inside Abbeystrewry church which says: 'During the period of famine his labours were unceasing; through his advocacy much relief was procured for the famished poor'.

THIS TABLET HAS BEEN ERECTED BY THE INHABITANTS
OF THIS TOWN AND NEIGHBOURHOOD TO THE MEMORY OF THE

REV. RICHARD BOYLE TOWNSEND,

32 YEARS VICAR OF ABBEY-STRAWRY.

A FAITHFUL AND ZEALOUS SERVANT OF HIS LORD, THE PRECEPTS
OF THAT GOSPEL WHICH HE BOLDLY PREACHED, HE CONSTANTLY PRACTISED.
DURING THE PERIOD OF FAMINE HIS LABORS WERE UNCEASING;
THROUGH HIS ADVOCACY MUCH RELIEF WAS PROCURED FOR THE FAMISHING POOR
THIS CHURCH WAS ENLARGED, AN ORGAN ERECTED, A SCHOOL-HOUSE BUILT
AND ENDOWED BY HIS ZEAL AND ACTIVITY.
HE ENTERED INTO HIS REST, MAY THE 7TH 1850, AGED 55 YEARS.
HE DIED OF FEVER, CAUGHT IN THE DISCHARGE OF DUTY.
THE SORROW EXPRESSED BY ALL CLASSES OF THE COMMUNITY WAS UNPRECEDENTED.
HE DIED AS HE HAD LIVED-IN FAITH.

BLESSED ARE THE DEAD WHICH DIE IN THE LORD,
EVEN SO SAITH THE SPIRIT, FOR THEY REST FROM THEIR LABORS.

Rev. R.B. Townsend's death from typhus in 1850 is commemorated by this plaque inside his parish church at Abbeystrewry. Townsend petitioned on behalf of the poor in Skibbereen and visited London in late 1846 where he met with Trevelyan. In January 1847 he wrote an open letter to the Archbishop of Canterbury in which he said: 'Thus, my Lord Archbishop, are we all in danger of our lives by the foetid and infected atmosphere we live in; from the walking poor compelled to roam about for help in fever, conveying infection to our very doors; or tainting it by laying unburied, in masses unknown, in their houses'.[3]

Chronic dysentery, also known as 'starvation dysentery', was at its peak during the winter of 1846-7. This was due to the unsuitable foodstuffs that people were forced to resort to, much of it from the hedge or shoreline. But Peel's 'Indian Meal' also caused problems. Irish people were unfamiliar with this type of food and it was often not prepared properly. This caused chronic diarrhoea which Dr Jones Lamprey of Schull described as 'pure blood and mucus', hence its other name, the 'bloody flux'.[4]

Disease raged throughout the Famine in many different forms. It was during 1847 that famine fever, dysentery and diarrhoea caused most deaths but they also persisted at extremely high levels throughout 1850.

Other common afflictions included tuberculosis, bronchitis, measles, influenza and scarlatina. The dreaded Asiatic cholera also struck pandemically in 1848-9.[5]

Disease was the major cause of death during the Great Famine.

J.W. Clerke was manager of the Provincial Bank in Bridge Street at the time of the Famine. He was very active in relief works and was a founder member of the Committee of Gratuitous Relief which set up the soup kitchen in Ilen Street. He was struck by fever in 1847 and his replacement at the bank gives us a very vivid account of conditions in the town in March 1847:

> The sub-inspector of police, who lives next door to the bank, is very bad today; some of the family of Dr. Donovan, a respectable medical man here, are also very ill; the wife of the Rev. Mr. Webb is despaired of; the manager of the National Bank was taken ill yesterday; the people of the hotel where I am staying have their children laid up; and, in short, the whole town and neighbourhood is in a lamentable state, resulting from famine and pestilence.
>
> At the moment that I write the bank door is surrounded by a crowd of starving creatures, craving assistance, and having all the appearance of disease. We are obliged to employ a person to stand at the door during business hours, to prevent their filling up the office; and one cannot walk through the street without being besieged by them. I assure you the scenes of misery that meet the eye on every side are most distressing; this very day two persons were found dying in the public street.[6] (Sketch of the present-day building by Cecilia Scholte Lubberink.)

While the majority of people died from disease, many more suffered through the long, slow, painful process of death by starvation. Dr Dan wrote about the effects of starvation on the body: 'the face and limbs become frightfully emaciated; the eyes acquire a most peculiar stare'. This was also described by the American visitor, Elihu Burritt, who wrote about a baby 'with clear, sharp eyes that did not wink but stared stick still at vacancy'.[7]

Eyewitnesses describe 'walking skeletons' who were literally skin and bone – 'had their bones been covered with a veil of thin muslin, they would not have been more visible'.[8]

Dr Dan described the pain of the sufferers and the 'feeling of weakness and sinking, accompanied by an insatiable thirst' and 'a distressing feeling of coldness over the entire surface of the body'.[9]

Though under-recorded, death from starvation was generally described as 'famine dropsy' or 'hunger oedema' by medical authorities.[13]

'Famine oedema' occurs at the final stages of death by starvation. The body starts to retain fluid and swell in certain places. Children take on a wizened and shrunken appearance and start to look like old men.[10] Burritt told of how a child's 'cold, naked arms were not much larger than pipe stems, while its body was swollen to the size of a full-grown person ... [and] the deepest lines of old age furrowed its face'.[11] Another distressing account tells of 'a man who had been at work on one of the roads, whose legs swelled to an enormous size, and when they burst, there was a copious discharge of pure water, that relieved him of suffering and life together'.[12]

Starvation caused huge psychological effects too, and resulted in people doing things that were far removed from their normal realm of behaviour. Dr Dan said that this was an 'inevitable consequence of starvation' when he vividly described this phenomenon:

> Another symptom of starvation ... is the total insensibility of the sufferers to every other feeling except that of supplying their own wants. I have seen mothers snatch food from the hands of their starving children; known a son to engage in a fatal struggle with a father for a potato; and have seen parents look on the putrid bodies of their offspring without evincing a symptom of sorrow.[14]

Dr Dan wrote of how starvation caused in many 'a state of imbecility' and in some 'almost complete idiotism'. Many contemporary reports from Skibbereen are about people driven to commit extreme acts by starvation.

> One man demanded to have his brother attended to who was a raving maniac, threatening to destroy the whole family; and this was induced from want of a sufficient supply of food.[15]

As is the case in the famines of the twenty-first century, it was the most vulnerable in society who were worst affected during the Great Hunger: the poor, the young, the old and the weak. Locheramoe Kuwom during the Kenyan Famine of 2011. (Photo: Eoghan Rice / Trocaire)

EVICTIONS

As the Famine progressed, more and more people fell into rent arrears. The new Poor Law of 1847 included a provision, 'the quarter-acre clause', which offered a method of clearing such unwanted tenants from the land. It was also known as the Gregory Clause because it was proposed by Lord William Gregory, landlord of Coole Park near Gort, as an additional clause to the poor law legislation of March 1847.

Under this clause, no one holding more than a quarter-acre of land could be admitted to the workhouse. When challenged about the wholesale devastation that it would unleash, Gregory said that '[if] the operation of a clause of this kind would destroy all the small farmers ... I do not see of what use such small farmers could possibly be'.[1]

Landlords were also liable for the rates of any tenant whose holding had a rateable valuation of under £4.[2] This was another incentive for landlords to clear their land of tenants who were not paying rent.

Some of the largest estate clearances in Cork took place in the Skibbereen Union where, newspapers reported, evictions were more numerous than in any other district.[3] Many of these were as a result of amendments to the poor laws in early 1847 under which anyone holding more than a quarter acre of land could not be admitted to a workhouse. ('Eviction Scene' by Daniel McDonald. Courtesy of the Crawford Art Gallery.)

49

The *Cork Examiner* carried a report of 370 people evicted in Gubbeen townland in November 1848, *c.* 25km west of Skibbereen, and included this notice for another proposed eviction:

'Take notice that I intend to dispossess the following persons, at present residing on the lands of Farnagulla ... in the Skibbereen Union, November 16, 1848. Patrick Leahy, John Leahy, Joanna Donovan, widow; Margaret Donovan, widow; John Donovan, Peter Donovan, Denis Martin, Margaret Coghlan, widow; Timothy Donovan, Mary Donovan, widow; Mary Sullivan, widow; Mary Neill, widow; Catherine Neill, widow. T. H. Marmion, agent to the Rev. M. F. S. Townsend'.[4]

Another distressing report from Gubbeen tells of the sad fate of Michael Crowley and his family. Mr Crowley had been employed on the road works at Lowertown but had been 'put off' and was 'extremely distressed, wandering from house to house in search of food'. Finally, in desperation, he brought his family into his house and built up the door with loose stones. His little boy crept through the crevices in the stones in search of food. He was offered some food by a neighbour, but said that his father needed it more. The neighbour returned to the house with him to find that Mr Crowley had 'built himself in with his family, that they might all lie down and die together'.[5]

Ruin at Gubbeen. (Photo: K. O'Regan)

Evictions often involved the demolition of the houses of those evicted. This prevented the former tenants from returning and sometimes cleared the land for 'improving tenants'. Quite often the houses were, at the very least, unroofed.

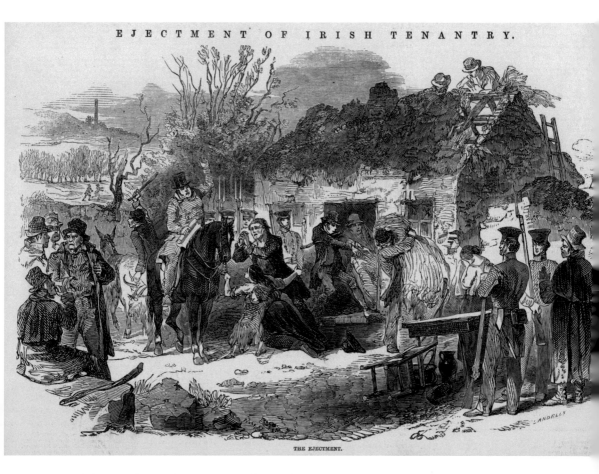

EJECTMENT OF IRISH TENANTRY.

THE EJECTMENT.

'Eviction of tenants for non-payment of rents – has been carried on to an extent that I could scarcely credit ... in ... the Catholic parish of Skibbereen ... [on] the property of Sir William Becher, the clearance system has been carried on to an alarming extent ... In North and South Ballinard ... the property of Mr. Akins, of Cork, the clearances have been numerous ... Innisbeg ... the property of James Murrough, Esq., Hyde Park, Cork, all the tenants were turned out, except four or five and a few labourers.'[6] (*ILN*. Image courtesy of Ireland's Great Hunger Museum, Quinnipiac University, Hamden, CT.)

Over the years of the Famine and shortly thereafter, about half a million people were put out of their homes.[7] With the workhouses full, many of them had nowhere to go.

People walked to towns and villages in search of aid. Many more simply walked while they still had strength, not knowing what else to do and these people 'on the roads' helped the spread of disease.

J.H. Swanton (see page 55) described people on their way to the workhouse, which was then actually closed:

> I saw some groups of families today crawling towards the workhouse, whose appearance almost broke my heart — fine frames, decent, well-conducted people — but actually starved into the workhouse and out of their own homes. One or two particularly were crying silently as they moved silently along.[8]

We perish houseless, naked, starved, with branded brow ...

Dying, dying wearily, with a torture sure and slow—

Dying, as a dog would die, by the wayside as we go.[9]

Evicting the Widow Ganey

In May 1847, 21 families were evicted from their homes in the townland of Highfield, *c.* 5km outside Skibbereen. Over 100 people were made homeless as a result. The *Cork Examiner* reported on the event, giving a list of those evicted which included farmers, labourers and the widow Ganey with her seven children.

The reporter Jeremiah O'Callaghan describes what he saw when he visited the site just after the eviction:

> [the agent] ascended the roof and [stripped] off the thatch ... The fever-stricken mother ... followed him for about a mile ... [and] endeavoured to crawl back but ... had no recourse but a ditch, where I saw her this day, apparently lifeless. I imagined she was a corpse ... but discovered she breathed slowly ... and discovered a child dying by her side. [10]

He created a 'sort of shed' with some broken furniture and left her and her child to die. His report of the following week says:

> She expired in the open air, with the exception of the few sticks before mentioned ... her death has occasioned considerable alarm in the locality. [11]

O'Callaghan reports that, on his first visit, he

> proceded [sic] through the deserted village to where the rest of her family lay ... laboring in all the agony of fever ... [where] a female spectre just risen from fever was bringing water to quench their thirst. [12]

She expired in the open air

"The townland of Highfield, in the parish of Creagh, is the property of Robert Dalacour Beamish Esq. of Cork. A few days since these proscribed victims were visited by the Rev. Summerset Townsend and Mr Lovel, agent and under agent to Mr. B., for the purpose of clearing these lands of the tenants. On that day, and some time prior, they succeeded in turning out the following persons with their families:

Daniel Whoulahane, farmer, with six in family.

Thomas Whoulihane, farmer, with six in family.

Michael Whoulahane, farmer, five in family.

Michael Ganey, labourer, three in family.

Widow Burke, five in family,

Denis Cartny, farmer, eight in family.

John Collins, farmer, eight in family.

John Sullivan, farmer, eight in family.

Florence Sullivan, farmer, seven in family.

Florence Carthy, farmer, three in family.

William Leahy, farmer, six in family.

Jeremiah Toomy, labourer, nine in family.

Michael Wholahan, farmer, ten in family.

Tom Croston, labourer, eight in family.

James Murphy, labourer, four in family.

Denis Cahalane, five in family.

Daniel Carthy, five in family.

Widow Donovan, five in family. At the moment of extermination, this ill-fated woman was preparing a little Indian Meal in a pot, which Lovel and Hosford threw out on the dung.

John Collins, labourer, died in the ruins of his own house.

The Widow Regan, four in family, subsequent to receiving notice to quit, had her husband and daughter laid out on the same table.

The Widow Ganey with seven in family.

Excerpt from the *Cork Examiner* of Monday evening, 31 May 1847.

Stark, in his *Journal* of 1850, said that 'Not a soul is now to be discovered in Highfield, a townland once densely populated, the property of Mr Delacour Beamish, ex M.P.' [13]

EMIGRATION

Emigration offered a chance to escape, and over 1.2 million people left Ireland between 1845 and 1851.[1] Emigration was already taking place prior to the Great Famine but the scale of the exodus during and post Famine was unprecedented in the history of international migration.[2] Over two million people left Ireland between 1845 and 1855, more than had emigrated from Ireland in the preceding two and a half centuries.[3]

In West Cork, where deaths were high, emigration was relatively low. People in the poorer areas simply did not have the means to leave and there was little 'assisted emigration'.

Plaque on a writing slope given to James H. Swanton of Skibbereen by 'Doctors Donovan, Somerville and Hadden' as a 'mark of regard and esteem'. Swanton offered 'assisted emigration' from Skibbereen in October 1846. Swanton was a miller who had a boat bound for England to collect a load of corn. He offered 100 people free passage on the empty outward journey. Dr Dan Donovan was authorised to grant 50 people a place on this voyage but soon had over 80 applicants. Many of them had pawned their clothes which Dr Dan redeemed. As they had no means of feeding themselves on the journey, the doctor got 2 shillings each for food from the local Relief Committee.[4] Swanton also set up a soup kitchen and 'more men would have died on the road near Ballydehob only for J. H. Swanton's soup-kitchen'.[5] (Photo: P. O'Regan, with thanks to Prof. Desmond Leddin.)

Emigration figures from Baltimore port show an exponential increase from 901 in 1845 to 2,122 in 1846.[6] *The Wanderer* sailed out of Baltimore on 23 December 1846 with '113 destitute passengers' and finally arrived in Wales on 1 February 1847, with 26 'men, women and children ... in a dying state stretched upon a scanty portion of straw'.[7]

'Wretched Condition of Emigrants', *Monmouthshire Merlin*, 6 February 1847. (Courtesy of John Sweeney, Chairman of the 'Wales Famine Forum', publishers of the *Green Dragon*.)

WRETCHED CONDITION OF EMIGRANTS.

Hundreds of unfortunate creatures from the land of famine have been recently thrown upon our shore, and the numbers increase so rapidly that the suggestion of a highly influential gentleman in our neighbourhood should be immediately adopted,—namely, a memorial to government, to meet the serious expense of sustaining these unhappy creatures, a course which has been adopted by the authorities at Liverpool, and which the Home Office cannot reasonably refuse; but in the mean time the wretched strangers must be taken care of and not suffered to perish.

On Monday last, a vessel called the *Wanderer*, Capt. Casey, from Baltimore, Ireland, arrived in this port, which place she left on the twenty-third of December last, with 113 destitute passengers, consisting of men, women, and children, several of whom were from Skibbereen: owing to adverse winds the vessel was obliged to put into Monkstown; they were then driven back again to Cork, and once more were they obliged to put into Monkstown, from which port they sailed, and finally reached here as before stated, but human conception can scarcely reach the depth of misery in which a large number of them appeared.

They were straitened for provisions, although we learn that the relief committee of Cork were not wanting in affording proper aid when the *Wanderer* put in there.

Men, women, and children, to the number of twenty-six were found in a dying state stretched upon a scanty portion of straw which but partially protected them from the hard and damp ballast on which they were lying in the hold. This sad fact being known upon the arrival of the ship at the wharf at Pillgwenlly,—the offices of humanity were promptly afforded by Mr. Honey, Mr. Pyne, and Mr. Jefferies, surgeon, and shortly after by a gentleman of the Subscription Fund Committee of Newport, but above all, the most prompt and efficacious assistance was rendered in the way of proper nourishment by the Misses Homfray and Mrs. Lewis. How true it is said of the tender sex,—

"When care and anguish wring the brow
A ministering angel thou."

We are happy to say, that through the prompt and assiduous care extended to those destitute people, but one death is likely to ensue, and the case of the survivors will be brought before the Board of Guardians at our Union to-morrow.

The Famine exodus started in earnest after the failure of the potato crop in August 1846. For the first time, desperate emigrants crossed the Atlantic in winter on sailing ships. By the spring of 1847, there was a panicked flight of frightened people leaving Ireland in huge numbers.

Three-quarters of those who sailed across the Atlantic left from Liverpool.[8] Thousands flocked to Liverpool causing huge problems of over-crowding and disease in the city. The media carried extensive coverage of this mass influx, with *The Times* describing the Irish in Liverpool as 'pestiferous'.[9] Over 5,000 Irish people died of fever in the city in 1847.[10] The *Illustrated London News* said of the treatment of the Irish by Liverpool parish officers: 'far more care would be taken of Irish cattle'.[11] Overall, it is estimated that up to 100,000 Irish Famine migrants died in Britain.[12]

The cheapest North American passages were to Canada, on ships that were very poorly regulated. Passengers experienced horrific conditions for up to six weeks on these 'coffin ships'. Over 100,000 wretched emigrants made this hazardous trip in 1847 and a third of them died on board ship or soon after landing.[13] Those with more resources travelled directly to New York or Boston. The poorest went to Liverpool in the hope of saving for a passage to America.

In the later years of the Famine, those who managed to emigrate sent home passage money for other family members. In 1848, this 'stream of gold' was half a million pounds, the following year this doubled and it continued to rise until the mid-1850s.[14] Extraordinary sacrifices were made by these early emigrants which allowed other family members to escape *an Gorta Mór*.

Many emigrants left the ports of West Cork on small ships during the Great Famine. Some of the poorest would only have the money to get as far as Britain. The massive surge of emigration in 1847 included middling farmers and others with resources who, bereft of hope, sold what they had left to escape the Famine. Their journey was full of hazards including robbery. 'Trappers', or confidence tricksters, hung around the ports to rob the unwary and illiterate travellers while 'runners' enticed them into so-called 'boarding houses' where they were robbed.[15] ('Emigrants Awaiting Embarkation West Cork' by Robert Richard Scanlan. Courtesy of the Crawford Art Gallery.)

Unlike Ireland, the destitute in Britain had a right to be provided with food under the Poor Law system. The influx of impoverished Irish into the ports of England, Scotland and Wales in 1847 put the local relief organisations under extreme pressure. To stop them becoming a permanent charge on the poor rates, Irish migrants dependent on poor relief were exported back to Ireland. About 15,000 paupers were removed from Liverpool in 1847 alone.[16]

Later Famine emigrants to Britain who were destitute on arrival and in need of relief were classed as vagrants and deported back to Ireland. As this poster from the Cardiff Union shows, a reward was given for information on ships that landed such desperate migrants illegally.

The flood of desperate, frightened, malnourished and often diseased, Irish people brought the consequences of the Famine to Britain's cities and towns. The constant stream of destitute migrants into the country hardened attitudes towards Irish landlords and the Irish poor themselves. The drastic changes to the Poor Laws in 1847 were an attempt to contain the poor in Ireland under the draconian edict of 'Irish property to support Irish poverty'.

Australian Orphans

While there was little 'assisted emigration' from Skibbereen, one international scheme did apply to the inmates of the workhouse. Proposed by Earl Grey, and named in his honour, this scheme sent 110 girls aged between fourteen and eighteen from Skibbereen Workhouse to Australia.[17]

These women were perceived as 'superfluous' and a drain on the Poor Law system in Ireland. However, in Australia there was a shortage of women, with eight men for every woman, and the colonial authorities were seeking to rectify this gender imbalance.[18]

The cost of the voyage to Australia from Britain was borne by the colonies but the local board of guardians was responsible for their passage to the UK port. They were to be supplied with six shifts, two flannel petticoats, six pairs of stockings, two pair of shoes, two gowns and a bible.[19] On arrival in Australia, these young Irish girls were indentured to employers as domestic servants for a defined period. The scheme finished in 1850 and, over the two years of its operation, 4,114 Irish girls were transported to Australia.[20]

Ellen Fitzgerald from Curragh, Skibbereen arrived in Australia in 1850 aged 17. She married a gold miner, William Newey, and they had 11 children. She died of a 'disability' at age 47.[22]

Some of these young women had difficult lives in the colonies. They had escaped a famine but faced new challenges in Australia. Many of them were ill-equipped for the work, having no experience in domestic service. The majority were illiterate and so were unable to record their stories. However, their experiences are not forgotten. The Australian National Memorial to the Great Irish Famine is inspired by the Irish Famine orphans and there is a database of records relating to them.[21]

A descendent of one of the Skibbereen 'orphan girls', Geoff Cummins, is pictured here with his wife Anne on their visit to Skibbereen Heritage Centre in 2015.

Geoff's great-great-grandmother, Mary O'Donovan, arrived in Melbourne in 1850 aged 19. She married her husband, Michael James Cummins, in 1852. Cummins was a Dublin-born master mariner who went on to establish himself as a timber and hardware merchant on the Ballarat goldfields where he also became a Town Councillor. He subsequently moved to the Geelong district where he was a merchant and farmer. In 1861, he became a member of the Victorian Legislative Assembly where he advocated social issues, including land reform. The 'Cummins Clause' was introduced into land legislation for the benefit of 'the poorer families'. Mary also worked on behalf of the poor. She was active in working for the 'widowed and the fatherless' in Ballarat and in support of the Orphanage and Convent of the parish of St Mary of the Angels. Mary died on 4 March 1866 at Ballarat aged 36. [23]

Skibbereen girl, 17 year old Mary Colgan [Coghlan?], arrived in Geelong in 1850. She married James Walton, a violent, drunken man who was convicted of manslaughter at the Ballarat gold diggings in 1857. Five years later she died from complications after a miscarriage resulting from her husband's beatings. [24]

DEATH

Death was the ultimate outcome of the Great Famine and it is estimated that approximately one million people died in Ireland during the crisis. While the fate of almost every bag of 'Indian meal' was strictly documented by the British administration, there was no attempt to record the names of those who died during the crisis, nor the number of people.

J.J. Marshal was appointed as the Poor Law Inspector for Skibbereen in early 1847. He compiled a statistical report of those who died in the parishes of the Mizen peninsula during the worst months of the famine.[2] This is the only record of its kind to be compiled during the Great Famine. Like many others engaged in relief work, Marshal died of fever in January 1849 and is buried in Abbeymahon graveyard in Skibbereen.[3] (Photo: W. Casey)

In the Skibbereen Union, there was a population loss of over 37,000 people in the decade 1841-51.[1] The Famine victims left little in their wake. Of the thousands who died, we only know a few names. For the vast majority, their stories remain untold.

In nineteenth-century Ireland death was accorded much respect. The dead were waked and there were many customs and practices associated with death. During the Famine, people were ashamed to be seen burying their loved ones without a coffin or a shroud. They were also afraid to let it be known that fever was in the house. 'To make it known that the famine fever had visited your house was to put a ring of fire around it.'[4] So Famine burials were often carried out in secret, in the dead of night, at a mass grave.

There were three main burial grounds in Skibbereen town: Abbeystrowry 'Famine burial pits', Chapel Lane graveyard and the grounds of the Skibbereen Workhouse. While no records exist of the number of people interred in these mass graves, it is estimated that between 8,000 and 10,000 Famine victims are buried in Abbeystrowry alone.[5] In the overall Skibbereen Union, there are many more sites where Famine victims are buried, some of them unmarked and unrecorded.

Lord Dufferin gives us a description of the pits at Abbeystrowry in 1847: 'By these graves, no service had been performed, no friends had stood, no priest had spoken words of hope … the bodies have been daily thrown in … one over another, the uppermost only hidden from the light of day by a bare three inches of earth, the survivors not even knowing the spot where those most dear to them lay sleeping.'[6] (Photo: R. O'Regan)

IN MEMORY
OF THE VICTIMS OF
THE FAMINE 1845 - 48
WHOSE COFFINLESS BODIES
WERE BURIED IN THIS PLOT

Go ndéana Dia trócaire ar a n-anamacha

'There rest the mortal remains of many generations of the people of Scull [Schull]; ... the burial ground ... doubled in size in order to receive upwards of half of the population within its bosom in a single year; and yet all were not interred there: many found a grave in the fields nearest to which they died; many others, among the ruins of their dismantled cabins.' [7] (Photo: T. Kearney)

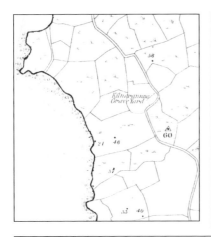

Many early church sites in Ireland would later be known as 'children's burial grounds' or 'cillíní', as they were used for burials of unbaptised infants when later Church law prohibited their burial in graveyards. Suicides, 'strangers' and seamen were also buried in such sites and they were also used during the Great Famine. 'Kilnaranna Graveyard' near Ballydehob is a 'Kill' or 'cillín' where there are Famine burials. Later known as 'Reen Keel', this site is mentioned in the Schools' Folklore Collection.[8] Tim Harrington, the great-grandfather of the current owner, buried a neighbour there during the Great Hunger using 'two sacks'. Another local story tells of how a woman came to the shoreline from the surrounding hillsides in search of mussels and died there. She, too, was buried in this 'cillín' during *an Gorta Mór*. [9] (© Ordnance Survey Ireland/ Government of Ireland. Copyright Permit No. MP 001615)

A story about this graveyard at Drimoleague tells of a man called Ned Good whose job it was to bury the dead during the Great Hunger. He used a coffin with a hinged base through which the corpse would fall. The coffin was reused repeatedly. One day, school-children from the village of Meenies [sic] followed Ned to watch him burying a body. They saw the 'dead man' raise his arm but, to their horror, Ned struck the arm with his spade and continued to cover the body with clay. The children rushed to tell someone about this and the grave was dug up. The buried man, who was from Schull, was found to be still living. Ned Good was dismissed from his post.[10] (Photo: R. O'Regan)

'A man from this neighbourhood ... died in the parish of Caheragh, and his brother went to have his remains removed to Stouk burying place, near Ballydehob. He agreed to pay the carman two shillings in Ballydehob for bringing the corpse, rolled up in an old sheet; but when he came near the village he ran off. The carman was about leaving the dead body on the road, had it not been for the police coming on him at the time; they had the car driven up to the Priest's house, who got a coffin immediately made, and the police had him buried'.[11] (Photo: R. O'Regan)

'Fourteen persons were buried in Kilmoe church-yard on Sunday last, of whom eleven were deposited in the ground without coffins.'[12]

'A boy of the name of Sullivan, his mother wailing over him, lay dead on the public road, near the chapel, in the face of the whole congregation going to and returning from mass.'[13]

'We beseech the government "though with no friendly voice" to save the people from perishing. What do we say? — They are perishing already — and no adequate relief is interposed between them and death ... We cannot see the end of all this.'[14]

Kilmoe Graveyard. (Photo: R. O'Regan)

Buried Alive

One of the more horrific aspects of the Great Famine was the number of people who were buried alive. Dr Dan Donovan warned about this when he wrote in the *Dublin Medical Press:* 'from the influence of cold on those suffering from starvation, many may be buried alive whilst in a state of asphyxia'. [15]

Dr Dan told the story of how he rescued a girl from the 'dead-cart' at the Square in Skibbereen. She was being taken to the grave when he happened to pass by. He verified that she still breathed and she was taken to the hospital at the Workhouse where her 'life was preserved for seven or eight days'.[16]

'The Famine in Ireland – Funeral at Skibbereen'. *(ILN)*

Johnny Collins was another person who survived being 'buried alive' during the Famine. His story was told by the Fenian revolutionary Jeremiah O'Donovan Rossa. Collins was a regular visitor to Rossa's shop on Levis's Quay in Skibbereen just after the Famine (see pages 71-72).

Dr Dan Donovan told another story about a boy who 'was found after a cold night on the public footpath, stiff, and apparently dead: he was thrown into the parish coffin, conveyed to the graveyard and flung into the common pit; the heat of the coffin restored animation, and to the surprise and alarm of the bier carriers, the supposed corpse raised itself from its lifeless companions and walked away: the little fellow afterwards became an inmate of the workhouse'.[17]

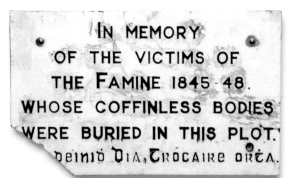

Another local man, Tom Guerin, was well known in the Skibbereen area as the 'boy who came back from the grave'. In the winter of 1848, when Tom was just two or three years old, he 'died' and was taken to Abbeystrowry where he was placed with the other bodies in the infamous Famine pits. The grave attendants were straightening the line of bodies to cover them with a light covering of straw or earth when they struck Tom across the knees with a shovel. The little boy whimpered and so they realised that he was alive. He was taken from the grave and lived on in the Skibbereen area until 1910. His knees were damaged during the interment and so Tom was 'a cripple' for the remainder of his life. But he used his notoriety to collect money at fairs and markets. We can get a sense of his wit from a poem that he composed:

I'm the poet, I'm the genius.

I rose from the dead in the year '48

When a grave near the Abbey had near been my fate,

Since then for subsistence I've done all my best,

Though one shoe points eastward and the other points west.

Skibbereen Eagle, 20 August 1910

DEATH OF TOM GUERIN.

INTERESTING LINK WITH THE PAST GONE.

Tom Guerin, so well known over Cork for the past half century, was interred in the Abbey graveyard on Saturday last. Every few of the general public —indeed if any—heard that "Poor Tom," as he was familiarly known, had passed away, so the funeral was by no means as representative as it would have otherwise been. By a peculiar coincidence, Tom was laid to rest in the same graveyard in which is erected a monument to the famine victims, the same graveyard in which he himself was buried alive in the dark days of "Black 48," and from which he was marvellously rescued after having had his legs broken by the shovels of the burial squad, who left him to his fate. Since his "resurrection"—as he was pleased to call it—Tom wandered the country round, and always got sufficient to prevent him from becoming a burthen on the rates. On one occasion

FAMINE - PEOPLE AND PLACES

Harrington's Hut

James Mahony of the *Illustrated London News* accompanied his sketch of 'Harrington's Hut' on 13 February 1847 with the following story:

> I started for Ballididicob [Ballydehob], and learned upon the road that we should come to a hut or cabin in the parish of Aghadoe [Aughadown], on the property of Mr Long, where four people had lain dead for six days; and, upon arriving at the hut, the abode of Tim Harrington, we found this to be true; for there lay the four bodies, and a fifth was passing to same bourne. On hearing our voices, the sinking man made an effort to reach the door, and ask for a drink or fire; he fell in the doorway; there, in all probability to lie; as the living cannot be prevailed to assist in the interments, for fear of taking the fever.

HARRINGTON'S HUT.

We hear more about the sad fate of the Harrington family from the *Cork Examiner:*

> In the parish of Aughadown, Tim Harrington died ... of hunger; malignant fever ... famine attacked the family and put a period to the painful sufferings of his son John; poverty and absence of friends obliged his brother to inter him in the *Cabbage Garden,* where he remained for eight days, his only sister Mary, dying of the same disease; at this time the benevolent subscribed for a coffin; the brother placed her in this and conveyed her to the next burial place where he *uncoffined her,* and proceeded home with the empty coffin; he then disinterred his brother; placed him in the same coffin and carried him back to the Grave yard.[1]

Unfortunately, there are no further records relating to the Harrington family of Aughadown and no knowledge exists of them today. However, baptism records of the parish show that Tim Harrington was baptised on 18 July 1825, his sister Mary on 5 January 1829 with parents Tim and Mary. John was sponsor for Mary's baptism. There is no baptism record for John, most likely because he was born before the records began in 1822. The family's townland is shown as 'Morrihane', now known as Murrahin.[2]

In the same Aughadown parish registers that recorded the Harrington family's baptisms, Fr Troy recorded in 1847: 'A Frightful famine and fever year alas! Hundreds dying with no marriages or baptisms'.

Jeremiah O'Donovan Rossa

Jeremiah O'Donovan Rossa was born in Rosscarbery in 1831. He had a very pleasant childhood but that all changed at the outbreak of the Great Famine in 1845. Within a few years, Rossa's father had died and his family had been evicted. All of his family went to America, but Rossa came to Skibbereen to live with an aunt.

The premises where O'Donovan Rossa traded as a general merchant on Levis's Quay Skibbereen is marked today with a mural of Rossa and a commemorative plaque. (Photo: P. O'Regan)

At just 17 years of age, Rossa had lived through all the horrors of the Famine, having had first-hand experience of hunger, disease, eviction, emigration and death.

Just a few short years after the Famine in 1856, Rossa and some other like-minded men formed the Phoenix National and Literary Society in Skibbereen. Two years later, James Stephens, one of the founders of the Irish Republican Brotherhood (IRB), travelled to Skibbereen to meet with Rossa and members of the Phoenix Society.

Rossa immediately joined Stephens' new movement and became one of its greatest advocates. A successful recruitment drive began in Skibbereen and spread throughout West Cork and south Kerry. Rossa went on to become one of Ireland's most famous revolutionaries.

Two episodes in his life above all else helped to create a heroic image of Rossa in the minds of the Irish people. These were his trial in 1865 and the appalling suffering he endured in English prisons from 1865 to 1870.

Following an amnesty, Rossa went to America in January 1871 and was very active in the Fenian movement, becoming one of its most hardline members.

Following his death on 29 June 1915, it was decided to bring Rossa's body home to Ireland for burial. A huge public occasion was planned by a new generation of Irish Nationalists and, as a gigantic propaganda exercise, Rossa's funeral to Glasnevin Cemetery on 1 August 1915 was a spectacular success.

Patrick Pearse delivered his famous oration and there's no doubt that it was a pivotal moment in the struggle for Irish independence.

Teampol na mBocht (Church of the Poor)

The term 'souperism' refers to the belief that people were only given relief if they gave up their Catholic faith and turned Protestant by 'taking the soup'. The vast majority of clergy, both Catholic and Protestant, freely gave relief without such conditions. Archdeacon Stuart in Aughadown, Rev. Caulfield in Creagh, Rev. R.B. Townsend in Skibbereen and others in Skibbereen Union dispensed soup from their homes as relief unconditionally.

One of those accused of souperism in the Skibbereen Union was the Rev. W.A. Fisher of Kilmoe parish. Fisher was responsible for the building of a church, *Teampol na mBocht* (Church of the Poor), in Altar townland near Schull as a Famine relief scheme in 1847.

The controversy arises because of a significant rise in the number of converts in that parish, explained by some as due to the alleged absence of the parish priest at that time.[3] Whether or not he was guilty of the charge of souperism, Fisher undoubtedly 'organised the distribution of large supplies of food and thus saved many lives'.[4]

Rev. Fisher raised money for Famine relief in Kilmoe and used it to build this church in 1847, to create local employment. To ensure that the work was done by labourers and not farmers, 'no horses were employed in it, all the work was done by hand'. (Photo: R. O'Regan)

Before the Famine, Fisher established the Crookhaven Loan Fund. Its aim was to provide credit to the poor of the area based on social capital, similar to one set up by J.W. Clerke in Skibbereen. It provided over a thousand small loans over its three years of operation. The records associated with the 'follow up' to these loans show that 100 out of the 309 people who availed of the scheme died in 1847.[5] This was an area which was clearly in need of aid and Fisher himself wrote that 'during the famine scarcely any persons perished in the hamlets near the church'.[6] This is borne out by the records of the loan funds which show no deaths for that townland.[7]

(Photo: T. Kearney)

Teampol na mBocht and Rev. Fisher feature in *Souper Sullivan,* a play by Eoghan Harris which is set in Famine times. It was staged at the Abbey Theatre as part of the Dublin Theatre Festival in 1985.

Schull Workhouse

Later in the Famine, the Skibbereen Union was reduced in size with the opening of the Clonakilty and Schull workhouses. The Union of Schull was officially formed in 1850.

By 1851, the population of Schull Workhouse was 1,311 while that of Schull village was 535.[8]

The Gregory Clause (see page 49) required tenants to give up their land in order to qualify for relief from the Workhouse. This caused untold misery and the story of Peter and Margaret Driscoll gives an insight into its operation as the Relieving Officer W.D. Williams testified:

> Peter Driscoll did apply to me for out-door relief, which I refused, knowing him to be in possession of a farm of land ... I then told him that on his producing me a certificate from the landlord of his giving up the possession, that I would give him outdoor relief, he being old and infirm. I heard nothing about him until I heard that he was carried dead to the town of Schull ... immediately after Driscoll's death his wife, Margaret Driscoll did apply for out-door relief, and told me that her husband was dead. I then inquired if she or he had given up the land, to which she replied that they had not, but that he went to give it up. I told her that she could not be relieved either inside or outside the workhouse as long as she held the land.

Margaret Driscoll went to get the necessary paperwork from the landlord's agent but Williamson heard no more from her. Her inquest heard that she had died 'from old age, exhaustion and exposure to cold'.[9] (Photo: T. Kearney)

Heir Island Shooting

On Christmas Eve 1848, *The Susan,* a vessel laden with wheat, was wrecked on a rock just off Reen point on Heir Island in Aughadown. For the starving people of the island, it was a God-send and crowds assembled to collect the cargo washed inshore. Five Coastguards from Baltimore and a policeman were called upon to guard the site. A crowd of up to 150 desperate islanders gathered on the rocks to plunder the bounty washed inshore. An altercation ensued and one of the Coastguards, George Moore, shot and killed an islander John Murphy.[10]

Reen, Heir Island (Photo: T. Kearney)

'Meinies'

As the pre-Famine population of Ireland increased, farms were repeatedly divided up. As a consequence, large extended family groups quite often lived together in the same area in clusters of houses known as 'claháns'. These 'villages' were scattered throughout West Cork like this one, 'The Village of Meinies' near Drimoleague, sketched by James Mahony in 1847.

(*ILN*, Courtesy of Ireland's Great Hunger Museum, Quinnipiac University, Hamden, CT.)

Mahony went to visit Meinies village because of a report from Dr Donovan that had appeared in the *Southern Reporter* a few weeks previously about a man called Leahey who had died in the village. 'His wife and two children remained in the house until the putrescent exhalations from the body' drove them from the house. A 'day or two after, some persons in passing the man's cabin, had their attention attracted by a loud snarling, and on entering, found the gnawed and mangled skeleton of Leahey'.[11] The remains of poor Mr Leahey had been eaten by dogs.

'[In] Mienies *[sic]* 80 individuals have perished out of 280.'[12]

Nothing remains of the village of Meinies today other than the remains of a road and the encircling walls. (Photo: R. O'Regan.)

Ballydehob 1847 and Now

This report from the *Cork Examiner* about conditions in Ballydehob is from January 1847:

> On Sunday last a man was found dead at Gubbeen, who dropped on the road-side on the previous night returning from one of the roads where he was employed under the Board of Works ... In the parish of Kilmoe a man was found dead in a field, and a great part of his body eaten by the dogs; he remained so long there before he was seen, that he was not identified by any person ... The following is an extract from a letter from Ballydehob, parish of East Skull: 'A poor man named Lenihan died on the road one or two days ago, and his wife got three shillings from the Revd. Mr. Barry to procure a coffin for him; she refused giving up the money to buy the coffin, fearing that she and the two little children would starve if she parted with the money; and the husband had to be buried by subscription this day'.

(ILN)

[In Ballydehob] the destitution was so frightful a nature that such persons as could command five pounds were leaving the town, to avoid the contagion of fever, as well as the afflicting scenes of persons dropping around them daily; and the informant added that the town was more than five times fuller of people from the surrounding countryside than it had accommodation for.[13]

(Photo: R. O'Regan)

Schull 1847 and Now

James Mahony reported from the village of Schull in 1847:

> We next got to Skull, where ... we witnessed almost indescribable in-door horrors. In the street, however, we had the best opportunity of judging of the conditions of the people; for here, from three to five hundred women, with money in their hands, were seeking to buy food; whilst a few of the Government officers doled out Indian meal to them in their turn. One of the women told me she had been standing there since daybreak, seeking to get food for her family at home. This food, it appeared, was being doled out in miserable quantities, at 'famine prices', to the neighbouring poor, from a stock lately arrived in a sloop, with a Government steam ship to protect its cargo of 50 tons; whilst the population amounts to 27,000; so that you may calculate what were the feelings of the disappointed mass.[14]

(ILN)   SKULL, FROM THE BALLIDCHOB.

In February 1847, around the same time as Mahony's sketch appeared in the *Illustrated London News*, a ship came into Schull delivering aid from the Society of Friends. We had this description given by the ship captain Commander Caffyn:

> Never in my life have I seen such wholesale misery, nor could I thought it so complete ... bodies half eaten by rats ... two dogs last Wednesday being shot by Mr O'Callaghan whilst tearing a body to pieces ... These are things which are of everyday occurrence.[15]

(Photo: R. O'Regan)

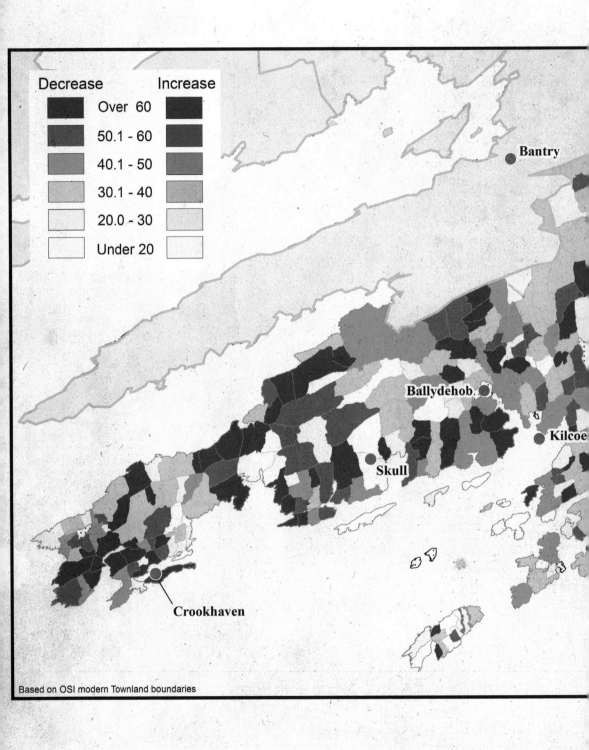

Decrease   Increase

Over 60

50.1 - 60

40.1 - 50

30.1 - 40

20.0 - 30

Under 20

Bantry

Ballydehob

Kilcoe

Skull

Crookhaven

Based on OSI modern Townland boundaries

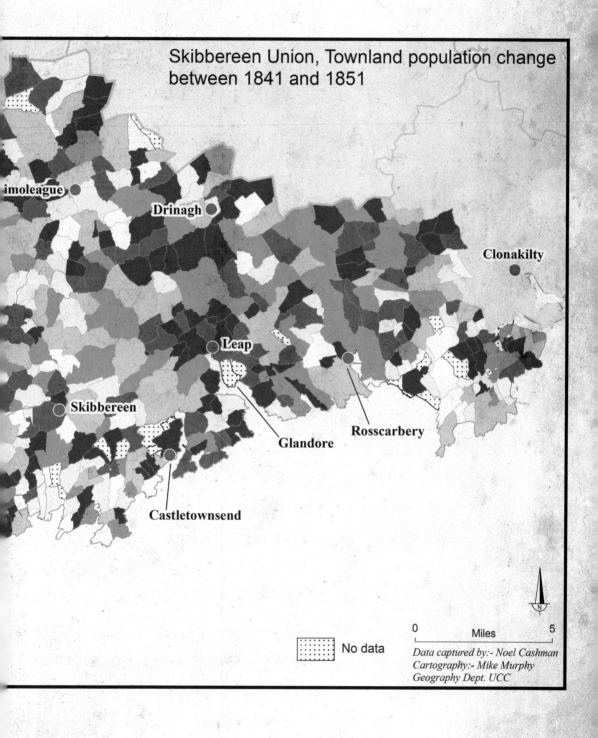

Skibbereen Union, Townland population change
between 1841 and 1851

imoleague

Drinagh

Clonakilty

Leap

Skibbereen

Rosscarbery

Glandore

Castletownsend

No data

0   Miles   5

Data captured by:- Noel Cashman
Cartography:- Mike Murphy
Geography Dept. UCC

The Final Word

Lived in the townland at the time as a tailor in poor circumstances.
Now in the city of Cork doing well.
(Peter O'Brien, Schull.)

Gone to America, he was in poor circumstances.
(George Driscoll Snr., Baltimore.)

Held a small farm, died 1847.
(John Coughlan, Bawnagollopy.)

Held a small hut, lived by begging, left the country in 1846.
(Eliza Walsh, Carrigtishane.)

Held a house and small plot of land.
Died in the Workhouse in '48, very poor.
(John Walsh, Aghills.)

Resides on the land, as a servant with her brothers.
At present in Skibbereen and lives by dealing in fish.
(Cath. Regan, Currabeg.)[1]

Over the years, working in Skibbereen Heritage Centre, we have met many, many thousands of people whose ancestors left Skibbereen during the Great Famine. While it is not possible to tell them all, we have heard stories of success, of torment, of alcoholism and of bravery.

The succeeding generations have prospered, as has the country of Ireland. However, we owe this success to those who went before us. Most especially those who endured the tragedy of the Great Famine in Skibbereen.

This book is in their honour, including John Kearney of Lissalohorig, Skibbereen.